Keto Diet Instant Pot Cookbook

Amazingly Simple Keto Diet Instant Pot Recipes To Live On the Keto Lifestyle, Lose Weight And Feel Great

Emma Saunders

Warning-Disclaimer

The purpose of this book is to educate and entertain. The author or publisher does not guarantee that anyone following the techniques, suggestions, tips, ideas, or strategies will become successful. The author and publisher shall have neither liability or responsibility to anyone with respect to any loss or damage caused, or alleged to be caused, directly or indirectly by the information contained in this book.

Table of Contents

Introduction

Health is one of the greatest gifts we are given, and to enjoy it longer, we have to control our meals just like we control our minds. Although good health brings peace and happiness to any family, nowadays, our society is ruled by artificial meals and lack of nutritional discipline, so it is hard to make the best choices when it comes to meals and healthy habits. People avoid spending time cooking and prefer to buy fast foods.

Fortunately, the Instant Pot cooking method offers a sensible, healthy, and quick solution. It is characterized as being ergonomic, convenient, and versatile. Instant Pot cooking has existed for many years, and even though we have old school pieces of machinery in our kitchens, such as microwaves, the Instant Pot remains one of the healthiest and fastest ways to cook food. unlike the microwave, where the food properties and vitamins are almost completely destroyed by the radiation.

The use of the Instant Pot can easily replace your slow cooker and traditional oven. So what is the Instant Pot and what can you cook with it? But before we proceed with the specifics of the Instant Pot Pressure Cooker, let's take a look at the Ketogenic Diet and it's benefits.

What is the Ketogenic Diet?

The Ketogenic diet is diet based on the variation of vegetables, meat, seeds and nuts that are known for being full of healthy nutrients such as vitamins, minerals, and most importanly antioxidants. And just because they are considered to be healthy, it doesn't mean they are difficult to prepare. I bet that you will find really easy to do it with this cookbook. Numerous researchers and scientists have discovered that the antioxidants present in "keto diet" are healthy molecules that protect and repair the cells from free and harmful elements such as free radicals. These are usually found in big quantities in the fried foods, red meats, dairy products, artificial sweeteners, soft drinks, and fast foods.

Where does the name "ketogenic" come from? It's very simple - when you go low on carbs, your body sends a message all over it that the primary source of energy has decreased and it must find another way of using up energy. Therefore, the next natural source of energy in your body are the fats. This process is called "ketosis" and it means that you enter in a state where you effectively burn fat as your main fuel.

How does it look like to be on the ketogenic diet? The answer is very simple, you will have to remove almost all kinds of food that is high in carbs and sugars. Yeah, no more pasta bolognese or sunday pancakes. Well, at least not in the way you used to it. However, this cookbook you more than make up for this change and you will find the transition to be almost unnoticeable.

Pros of the Keto Diet

Control Your Weight

The ketosis process that I expained above, makes the body to use the already stored fat as a primary source of energy, which automatically means that you will become leaner. Another benefit is that the low consumation of carbs, already is key to a significant weight loss. So if you've got a lot of belly to lose, welcome the good news. Not only, you will lose fat on the outside, but most importantly, you will be removing fat from around your organs, and that's awesome news for your overall health, easier than ever to exercise and to recover.

With all this being said, here are some of the main benefits of the ketogenic diet.

Effeciency and Cost Reduction

The less carbs your consume, the more money you will save. Imagine leaving all the sweets, alcohol, expensive breads, etc. out of your carriege? That's a huge saving, both in short and long term. And you will be healthier? Thta's no brainer.

Burst of energy

Many people who follow the keto diet report that they are much more energetic and less tired than before. That's easily explainable by the fact that you are not giving your body constant doses of carbohydrates and sugars. This leads to much less frequent insulin spikes (also known as sugar spikes) in your blood sugar. You will find out that you no longer feel slow and tired, especially in the afternoon, and your are much more clear minded and concetrated.

What to Consume on the Keto Diet:

- Fats and Oils

- Protein

- Vegetables

- Dairy (Full-fat if possible)

- Nuts and Seeds

What to Avoid on the Keto Diet:

- Grains

- Beans and Legumes

- Most Fruits - that includes fruit juices, smoothines and dried fruits

- Sugars and Soft Drinks

What is the Instant Pot?

If your life is constantly happening on left lane and you have to do things on the run, including cooking, then Instant Pot is designed for you. In a few words, this kitchent appliance is a pressure cooker that provides a multitude of functions at the same time.

They are all programmable and customizable Instant Pot can do the work of seven appliances:

1. Pressure Cooker/Manual Mode

2. Slow Cooker

3. Porridge maker/Rice cooker

4. Sauté pan

5. Steamer

6. Serving/Warming pot

7. Yogurt Maker

Instant Pot - Pros and Cons?

The Pros

The exterior parts of the Instant Pot are characterized by their plastic composition, and they never come in contact with the meals that are prepared inside it. Therefore, no plastic particles end up in your food.

It is also a multi-use gadget and can replace a slow-cooker, a rice-cooker, a sauté-pan, and a steamer. It can be used so often, that the use of stoves and ovens becomes redundant.

The use of Instant Pot has gradually replaced the well-known slow cookers. This is mainly due to the quicker and more efficient work of the Instant Pot - it is also more practical, and in many of the cases, saves space.

Time Saving This is considered one of the greatest benefits for people who use the

Instant Pot. While sometimes you need at least 5 to 8 hours to cook in the slow cooker, with the Instant Pot you can prepare the meal in just 30 minutes. It is unbelievably helpful, especially on busy days or when you come back late from work/trip.

One of the major advantages of an Instant Pot is that it is programmable, something diffcult to fing in the regular pressure cookers or slow cookers. And because it cooks very quickly, you will notice that it allows you to program as early as 24-hours before the actual cooking taking place.

The Cons

The use of the Instant Pot is safer than the use of any other types of pressure cooker; however, it also releases steam and can cause burns if misused. Make sure to be careful when you use it. Place it in the back corner of your counter and make sure there are no chairs or stools and the kids are kept away. Also, make sure you read the instruction manual before your first use of an Instant Pot, and avoid contact to running water.

To sum up

There are over 150 different Instant Pot recipes - soups, breakfasts, sides, lunch, salads and desserts. If you consider yourself a person who loves eating healthy food, all you need is an Instant Pot. Even if you are not a cook at all, this book will help you prepare delicious meals. The recipes included are easy to prepare, and you will definitely enjoy them.

Breakfast Recipes

1.   Spanish Zucchini Frittata

(Time: 15 minutes \ Servings: 3)

INGREDIENTS:

3 eggs
1 large zucchini
1 onion, chopped
½ teaspoon thyme, chopped
¼ teaspoon salt
¼ teaspoon white pepper
2 tablespoons olive oil

DIRECTIONS:

- Cut the zucchini into thin strips and set aside.
- Crack the eggs in a medium bowl and whisk for 1 minute.
- Add the zucchini strips, onion, thyme, salt, and pepper, mix well.
- Add 3-4 cups of water into the Instant Pot and place a trivet or stand inside it.
- Now spray a medium-sized baking dish with olive oil, transfer the eggs mixture into a pan and place on a trivet. Seal the lid and cook on manual mode for 10 minutes. Once ready, serve hot and enjoy.

2.   Cheesy Spinach Casserole

(Time: 25 minutes \ Servings: 4)

INGREDIENTS:

1 cup spinach, chopped
half lb. cheddar cheese
half lb. mozzarella cheese
1 onion, chopped
4 eggs, whisked
l yellow bell pepper, chopped
¼ teaspoon salt
¼ teaspoon black pepper
2 tablespoons olive oil

DIRECTIONS:

- In a bowl add the eggs, spinach, mozzarella cheese, cheddar cheese, bell pepper, and onion, mix well.
- Season with salt and pepper. Grease the Instant Pot with olive oil.
- Transfer the spinach mixture to the Instant Pot and seal the lid.
- Cook for 25 minutes on slow mode. Once ready, carefully open the lid and serve immediately.

3.   The Easiest Eggs with Mushrooms

(Time: 15 minutes \ Servings: 3)

INGREDIENTS:

1 cup mushrooms, sliced
4 eggs
2 tomatoes, chopped
1 cup basil, chopped
1 teaspoon butter
salt and pepper, to taste

DIRECTIONS:

- Whisk eggs in a bowl. Add salt and pepper, tomatoes, basil and mushrooms. Mix well.
- Grease a round baking tray and pour the mixture into it.
- Place it in the instant pot, seal the lid and cook for 10 minutes on manual on high pressure.
- When done, enjoy the delicious mushroom treat!

4.   Healthy Artichokes with Eggs

(Time: 20 minutes \ Servings: 2)

INGREDIENTS:

2 cups artichokes, peeled
1 teaspoon fennel
2 teaspoon cream
3 egg s
4 garlic cloves, minced
1 teaspoon nutmeg powder
salt and pepper, to taste

DIRECTIONS:

- Whisk the eggs in a bowl.
- Add fennel, cream, nutmeg powder, salt and pepper.
- Blend well and then add artichokes.
- Pour the mixture into a round baking tray.
- Cook in the instant pot for 15 minutes on high pressure.
- When ready, serve and enjoy!

5. Ricotta Cheese with Eggs

(Time: 15 minutes \ Servings: 4)

INGREDIENTS:

4 eggs
½ cup stevia
2 ½ cups ricotta cheese
1 cup vanilla yogurt
2 teaspoon vanilla extract
½ cup white almond flour
1 teaspoon baking powder
2 cups sweet yogurt glaze
salt to taste

DIRECTIONS:

- Mix eggs, stevia, vanilla extract and flour in a bowl.
- Put it in the instant pot and mix with vanilla yogurt along with salt. Stir well.
- Add baking powder. Let it cook on high pressure for 10 minutes.
- When ready, take it out and serve it dressed with the sweet yogurt glaze.

6. Fresh Veggies Mix

(Time: 20 minutes \ Servings: 2)

INGREDIENTS:

½ cup full-fat milk
6 oz. chopped spinach
1 cup cheese, shredded
½ onion, chopped
½ bell pepper, chopped

4 eggs
Salt and pepper, to taste
½ cup mint, chopped
1 teaspoon oil

DIRECTIONS:

- Whisk eggs in a bowl.
- Add milk, cheese, spinach, onion, bell pepper, salt and pepper, and mint.
- Grease the round baking tray with oil. Pour the mixture into a tray.
- Let it cook in the instant pot for 14 minutes on high pressure. When done, serve and enjoy!

7.   Delicious Scallions and Eggs

(Time: 10 minutes \ Servings: 4)

INGREDIENTS:

2 eggs
1 cup water
½ lb. scallions, chopped
½ cup sesame seeds
½ tsp. garlic powder
salt and pepper, to taste

DIRECTIONS:

- Mix water and eggs in a bowl.
- Add scallions, sesame seeds, garlic powder, and salt and pepper in the instant pot.
- Add the egg mixture. Set the timer on manual for 5 minutes.
- When the timer goes off, quick release the pressure of the instant pot. Serve and enjoy!

8.   Clasic Eggs with Cheese and Bacon

(Time: 14 minutes \ Servings: 4)

INGREDIENTS:

5 eggs
½ tsp. lemon pepper seasoning
3 teaspoon cheddar cheese, grated

2 green onions, chopped

3 slices bacon, crumbled

DIRECTIONS:

- Whisk the eggs in a bowl and put them in the instant pot.
- Now mix the cheddar cheese, green onion and bacon with the eggs.
- Let it cook for 10 minutes on high pressure.
- When done, season it with lemon pepper and enjoy!

9.   Spinach and Tomato Cheesy Braise

(Time: 50 minutes \ Servings: 4)

INGREDIENTS:

1 cup baby spinach, sliced

2 tomatoes, chopped

1 cup mushrooms, sliced

1 teaspoon ginger powder

1 teaspoon garlic paste

¼ lb. parmesan cheese, shredded

½ lb. mozzarella cheese, shredded

1 egg, whisked

¼ pinch salt

¼ teaspoon thyme

¼ teaspoon black pepper

2 tablespoons butter, melted

DIRECTIONS:

- In the Instant Pot, add the butter and sauté garlic for 30 seconds on sauté mode.
- Add the spinach, tomatoes, thyme, salt, black pepper, egg, ginger powder, mozzarella cheese and mushrooms and mix well.
- Seal the lid and cook on slow cook mode for 45 minutes.
- Once ready, open the lid and sprinkle with the grated parmesan. Serve hot and enjoy.

10. Eggs Chicken Casserole

(Time: 30 minutes \ Servings: 4)

INGREDIENTS:

¼ lb. chicken breast, cut into small pieces
3 eggs, whisked
1 onion, chopped
3-4 garlic cloves, minced
½ lb. mozzarella cheese, shredded

2 oz. parmesan cheese
¼ teaspoon salt
¼ teaspoon black pepper
¼ teaspoon thyme
2 tablespoons butter

DIRECTIONS:

- Melt butter in the Instant Pot on sauté mode. Fry onion and garlic for 1-2 minutes.
- Add the chicken and fry until golden brown. Add salt, black pepper, thyme and mix well.
- Now add the eggs, parmesan cheese, mozzarella cheese and mix thoroughly.
- Seal the lid on and cook on high pressure for 20 minutes.

11. Creamy Eggs Casserole

(Time: 15 minutes \ Servings: 3)

INGREDIENTS:

4 eggs, whisked
1 onion, sliced
1 green chili, chopped
1 red bell pepper, chopped
½ lb. mozzarella cheese, shredded
¼ teaspoon salt
¼ teaspoon black pepper
¼ teaspoon dried basil
2 tablespoons butter

DIRECTIONS:

- Melt butter on sauté mode and sauté onion for 30 seconds.
- Now add the bell pepper and fry for a minute.
- Add the eggs, mozzarella cheese, green chilies, and season with basil, salt and pepper.
- Cover with a lid and cook on high pressure cook mode for 10 minutes.

12. Hot Scrambled Eggs

(Time: 15 minutes \ Servings: 2)

INGREDIENTS:

4 eggs, whisked
¼ teaspoon salt
1 cup chicken broth
¼ teaspoon black pepper
¼ teaspoon dill, chopped
2 tablespoons olive oil

DIRECTIONS:

- Heat oil in the Instant Pot on sauté mode and pour the whisked eggs.
- Crumble the eggs using a fork and add the chicken broth. Season with salt and pepper.
- When the chicken broth is dried out, transfer the scrambled eggs to a serving dish and top with dill.

13. Sweet Potato Casserole with Cream

(Time: 25 minutes \ Servings: 2)

INGREDIENTS:

2 sweet potatoes, peeled, sliced
1 cup mayonnaise
1 cup heavy cream
1 cup chicken broth
1 red onion, sliced
½ teaspoon chili powder
¼ teaspoon salt
2 tablespoons olive oil

DIRECTIONS:

- Heat oil in the Instant Pot on sauté mode and sauté onion for 1 minute.
- Now add the sweet potatoes and stir for 1-2 minutes.
- Add the chicken broth, and salt and cook on low heat for 20-25 minutes until the potatoes soften.
- Now stir in the mayonnaise and the heavy cream. Top with chili powder and serve.

14.   Benedict Asparagus Eggs

(Time: 20 Minutes \ Servings: 2-3)

INGREDIENTS

7 stalks of asparagus

5 eggs

2 tsp. of apple cider vinegar

chives for garnishing

2 teaspoon hollandaise sauce

2 egg yolks

¼ cup coconut oil

2 tsp. of fresh lemon juice

¼ tsp. of paprika

¼ tsp. of sea salt

DIRECTIONS

- Heat the Instant Pot and place the trivet inside it. Break each of the eggs into a small ramekin.
- Trim the asparagus stalks from the bottom.
- Slice the asparagus stalks lengthwise.
- Pour 1 cup of water into a sauce pan and cook the asparagus for 5 minutes.
- Place asparagus in each ramekin and add the cider vinegar.
- Slide the eggs in the ramekin, then cover the Instant Pot with a lid and set the feature to Soup, cooking the ingredients for 8 minutes.
- Prepare the sauce by boiling water in a blender, then cover and set aside for 10 minutes.
- Blend the egg yolk and add the lemon juice, the salt, and the paprika.
- Add the melted butter and keep mixing for 40 seconds.
- Serve each of the eggs over the dish of asparagus stalks and top with the hollandaise sauce and chives.

15.   Coconut Yogurt with Blueberries

(Time: 10 hours \ Servings: 6)

INGREDIENTS

2 lb. of coconut milk

2 tsp. of agar flakes

4 teaspoon of coconut yogurt

2 teaspoon of stevia

1 cup blueberries

½ cup strawberries

DIRECTIONS

- Pour the coconut milk into a cooking pot. Whisk the milk until it smoothens and add the thickener.

- Then sprinkle 1 tsp. of the agar flakes into the pot.
    - Warm the coconut milk.
    - Set to Manual and the timer to 5 minutes or until the milk begins simmering.
    - Whisk from time to time until you notice the agar agar are dissolved. Turn off the heat.
    - Add the probiotics and whisk to combine the ingredients. Add the stevia and whisk the ingredients again.
    - Add the blueberries and the strawberries on top and don't stir.
    - Lock the Pressure Valve. Use a lid made of glass.
    - Press the Yogurt button - you will see that the screen displays 8:00. Adjust it to 10:00.
    - The program will automatically finish after 8 hours. Let cool and enjoy!

Lunch and Dinner Recipes

16. Mexican Cod Fillets

(Time: 20 minutes \ Servings: 3)

INGREDIENTS:

3 cod fillets
2 cups cabbage
1 cup almond flour
½ teaspoon flaxseed meal
½ tsp. baking powder
Salt to taste
Juice from 1 lemon
1 Jalapeno pepper
½ tsp. oregano
½ tsp. cumin powder
½ tsp. cayenne pepper
2 teaspoon olive oil

DIRECTIONS:

- Put flour, flaxseed meal, salt, baking powder and lemon juice into a bowl. Mix well.
- If you need to add water, it can be added accordingly as well.
- Now mix cayenne powder, cumin powder and oregano in the mixture made in step 1.
- Stir well. Add oil into the instant pot and let the ingredients sauté.
- Add the cod fillets, jalapeno and cabbage over it.
- Pour the flour mixture into the pot and let it cook for 15 minutes. When done, enjoy the delicious meal!

17. Simple Mushroom Chicken Mix

(Time: 18 minutes \ Servings: 2)

INGREDIENTS:

2 tomatoes, chopped
½ lb. chicken, cooked and mashed
1 cup broccoli, chopped
1 teaspoon butter

2 teaspoon mayonnaise
½ cup mushroom soup
salt and pepper, to taste
1 onion, sliced

DIRECTIONS:

- Put chicken into a bowl.
- Mix mayonnaise, mushroom soup, tomatoes, onion, broccoli, and salt and pepper.
- Grease a round baking tray with butter. Put the mixture in a tray.
- Let it cook in instant pot for 14 minutes on high pressure. When ready, serve and enjoy!

18. Healthy Halibut Fillets

(Time: 15 minutes \ Servings: 2)

INGREDIENTS:

2 halibut fillets
1 teaspoon dill
1 teaspoon onion powder
1 cup parsley
2 teaspoon paprika
1 teaspoon garlic powder
1 teaspoon lemon pepper
2 teaspoon lemon juice

DIRECTIONS:

- Mix lemon juice, lemon pepper, garlic powder, and paprika, parsley and onion powder in a bowl.
- Add dill to it. Pour the mixture in the instant pot and place halibut fish over it.
- Let it cook for 10 minutes on high pressure. When ready, serve and enjoy!

19. Clean Salmon with Soy Sauce

(Time: 15 minutes \ Servings: 3)

INGREDIENTS:

2 Salmon fillets
½ maple syrup
2 teaspoon soy sauce

1 teaspoon garlic powder
salt and pepper, to taste

DIRECTIONS:

- Put maple syrup, soy sauce, salt, pepper and garlic powder into a bowl.
- Dip salmon in the mixture and place it in the instant pot. Let it cook for 10 minutes.
- When done, serve and enjoy!

20. Shrimp with Linguine

(Time: 20 minutes \ Servings: 2)

INGREDIENTS:

1 lb. shrimp, cleaned
1 lb. linguine
1 teaspoon butter
½ cup white wine
½ cup cheese, shredded
2 garlic cloves, minced
1 cup parsley
salt and pepper, to taste

DIRECTIONS:

- Put butter in the instant pot and let it sauté. Mix in linguine, white wine, cheese, garlic cloves and parsley.
- Let it cook for 4 minutes. Add shrimp and cook for 10 more minutes.
- When done, serve and enjoy!

21. Simple Salmon with Eggs

(Time: 10 minutes \ Servings: 3)

INGREDIENTS:

1 lb. salmon, cooked, mashed
2 eggs
2 onions
2 stalks celery
1 cup parsley, chopped
1 teaspoon oil
salt and pepper, to taste

DIRECTIONS:

- Mix salmon, onion, celery, parsley, and salt and pepper in a bowl. Put oil in the instant pot and let it sauté.
- Meanwhile, make patties out of the mixture and dip them in the whisked eggs.
- Place each patty in the pot when all are made, and let them cook for 5 minutes.
- When ready, enjoy the delicious fish patties.

22. Easy Shrimp

(Time: 13 minutes \ Servings: 2)

INGREDIENTS:

1 lb. shrimp
2 garlic cloves
2 teaspoon oil
1 teaspoon butter.
red pepper, a pinch
salt and pepper, to taste
1 cup parsley, chopped

DIRECTIONS:

- Put the shrimp into the instant pot and let them cook for 2 minutes.
- Add garlic cloves, oil, butter, red pepper, and salt and pepper. Let it cook for another 5 minutes.
- When ready, take it out and garnish with parsley.

23. Scallops with Mushroom Special

(Time: 24 minutes \ Servings: 2)

INGREDIENTS:

1 lb. scallops
2 onions , chopped
1 teaspoon butter
2 teaspoon oil
1 cup mushrooms
salt and pepper, to taste
1 teaspoon lemon juice

DIRECTIONS:

- Put oil into the instant pot. Add onions, butter, mushrooms, salt and pepper, lemon juice and scallops. Let it cook for 20 minutes on high pressure.
- When ready, it beeps, so take it out and serve!

24. Delicious Creamy Crab Meat

(Time: 15 minutes \ Servings: 3)

INGREDIENTS:

1 lb. crab meat
½ cup cream cheese
2 teaspoon mayonnaise
salt and pepper, to taste
1 teaspoon lemon juice
1 cup cheese, shredded

DIRECTIONS:

- Mix mayonnaise, cream cheese, salt and pepper, and lemon juice in a bowl.
- Add crab meat to it and make small balls.
- Place the balls in the instant pot and let them cook for 10 minutes on high pressure. When done, sprinkle the cheese over it and serve!

25. Tilapia Delight

(Time: 16 minutes \ Servings: 4)

INGREDIENTS:

4 tilapia fillets
4 teaspoon lemon juice
2 teaspoon butter
2 garlic cloves
½ cup parsley
salt and pepper, to taste

DIRECTIONS:

- Mix tilapia with lemon juice and put it into the instant pot.
- Add butter, garlic cloves, parsley, and sprinkle salt and pepper over it.
- Cover it and let it cook for 10 minutes.
- When ready, serve and enjoy this simple tilapia recipe.

26. Spinach Tomatoes Mix

(Time: 14 minutes \ Servings: 2)

INGREDIENTS:

2 teaspoon butter
1 onion, chopped
2 cloves garlic
1 teaspoon cumin powder
1 teaspoon paprika
2 tomatoes , chopped
2 cups vegetable broth
1 small bunch of spinach, chopped
cilantro for garnishing

DIRECTIONS:

- Add butter into the instant pot. Sauté it. Mix onion, garlic, and cumin powder, paprika, and vegetable broth. Stir well. Add tomatoes and spinach. Cook on high pressure for 10 minutes. When ready, enjoy!

27. Spinach Tortilla

(Time: 35 minutes \ Servings: 3)

INGREDIENTS:

1 cup almond flour
1 cup spinach, chopped
¼ teaspoon chili flakes
¼ cup mushrooms, sliced
½ teaspoon salt
1 cup cooking oil

DIRECTIONS:

- In a bowl, add the flour, the mushrooms, spinach, salt, and chili flakes and mix well.
- Add ¼ cup of water and make a thick batter. Heat oil in the Instant Pot and drop a spoon of butter.
- Transfer the mixture and cook until golden brown.
- Serve with cilantro sauce and enjoy.

28. Creamy Broccoli Stew

(Time: 45 minutes \ Servings: 4)

INGREDIENTS:

1 cup heavy cream
3 oz. parmesan cheese
1 cup broccoli florets
2 carrots, sliced
½ teaspoon garlic paste
¼ teaspoon turmeric powder
¼ teaspoon salt
¼ teaspoon black pepper
½ cup vegetable broth
4 tablespoon butter

DIRECTIONS:

- Melt butter in the Instant Pot on sauté mode.
- Add garlic and sauté for 30 seconds.
- Add the broccoli and the carrots, and cook until softened.
- Stir in the vegetable broth and cover with a lid.
- Cook on slow mode for 40 minutes.

29. Feta and Cauliflower Rice Stuffed Bell Peppers

(Time: 25 minutes \ Servings: 3)

INGREDIENTS:

1 green bell pepper
1 red bell pepper
1 yellow bell pepper
½ cup cauliflower rice
1 cup feta cheese
1 onion, sliced
2 tomatoes, chopped
1 teaspoon black pepper
2-3 garlic clove, minced
3 tablespoon lemon juice
3-4 green olives, chopped
3-4 tablespoons olive oil

DIRECTIONS:

- Grease the Instant Pot with olive oil.
- Make a cut at the top of the bell peppers near the stem.
- Place the feta cheese, onion, olives, tomatoes, cauliflower rice, salt, black pepper, garlic powder, and lemon juice into a bowl and mix well.
- Fill up the bell peppers with the feta mixture and insert in the Instant Pot.
- Set the on high pressure mode for 20 minutes.

Appetizers

30. Sweet Potatoes with Cheese

(Time: 15 minutes \ Servings: 4)

INGREDIENTS:

4 sweet potatoes, diced
3 garlic cloves, chopped
salt and pepper, to taste
½ cup parsley, chopped
½ cup sage, chopped
½ cup thyme, chopped
½ cup full-fat milk
2 teaspoon butter
½ cup shredded cheese

DIRECTIONS:

- Add sweet potatoes, salt and pepper, garlic cloves, sage, parsley, thyme and milk into the Instant Pot.
- Cook for 10 minutes on high pressure.
- Release the pressure and then add butter and cheese to it.
- Cook for another 5 minutes.
- When ready, serve and enjoy!

31. Avocado Paste Snack

(Time: 25 minutes \ Servings: 2)

INGREDIENTS:

2 avocados
¼ cup green bell pepper, diced
2 cup cucumber, diced
salt and pepper, to taste
2 teaspoon lime juice
2 teaspoon cilantro
1 cup water
¼ cup white vinegar

DIRECTIONS:

- Add avocados and green bell pepper into the pot.
- Mix in the cucumber and water. Cook for 5 minutes.
- Blend the mixture in an electric blender for 2 minutes.
- Put the mixture back into the same pot.
- Mix in lime juice, white vinegar, and salt and pepper.
- Cook for another 15 minutes on high pressure. When ready, garnish with cilantro to serve!

32. Delicious Chicken Broth Recipe

(Time: 9 minutes \ Servings: 4)

INGREDIENTS:

2 teaspoon butter
2 cups chicken broth
1 small pack harvest grain blend
a pinch salt and pepper

DIRECTIONS:

- Add chicken broth into the instant pot along with harvest grain package.
- Add butter along with salt and pepper,
- Cook for 5 minutes on high pressure. When ready, serve and enjoy!

33. Tomatoes Mix Recipe

(Time: 10 minutes \ Servings: 3)

INGREDIENTS:

1 teaspoon olive oil
1 onion, chopped
2 garlic cloves, minced
2 cup vegetable stock
2 tomatoes, diced
salt to taste
2 bay leaf
½ teaspoon oregano powder
½ teaspoon rosemary powder.
¼ cup basil

DIRECTIONS:

- Add olive oil in the instant pot and press the sauté button.
- Mix onion, tomatoes, vegetable stock, bay leaf, rosemary powder, salt, and oregano powder.
- Let it cook on high pressure for 5 minutes. When ready, serve with basil over it. Enjoy!

34. Eggs in Sausage

(Time: 20 minutes \ Servings: 4)

INGREDIENTS:

4 eggs
2 cups water
1 lb. ground sausage
4 teaspoon vegetable oil

DIRECTIONS:

- Place the eggs in the instant pot with water.
- Let them cook for 10 minutes.
- When boiled, take them out and peel off the skin.
- Now take each egg, cover it with the ground sausage, and shape it into a ball.
- Lightly brush the egg/sausage ball with vegetable oil.
- Place it in the instant pot.
- Do the same with all eggs.
- Let it cook in the instant pot for 10 minutes.
- When it beeps, serve and enjoy!

35. The Simplest Sweet Potatoes with Parsley

(Time: 13 minutes \ Servings: 3)

INGREDIENTS:

4 sweet potatoes, diced
2 cups water
2 eggs
1 onion, chopped
2 teaspoon mayonnaise
½ cup Parsley, chopped

½ cup dill pickle juice
1 teaspoon mustard
salt and pepper, to taste

DIRECTIONS:

- Add water and potatoes in the instant pot.
- Cook on high pressure for 3 minutes.
- Whisk the eggs and add them to the pot.
- Add onion, parsley, dill pickle juice, mayonnaise, mustard, salt and pepper.
- Mix well. Cook on high pressure for 5 minutes.
- When ready, serve and enjoy!

36. Sweet Potato Wedges

(Time: 25 minutes \ Servings: 4)

INGREDIENTS:

3 medium sweet potatoes, cut into wedges
1 teaspoon garlic powder
½ teaspoon cinnamon powder
½ teaspoon cumin powder
2 tablespoons lemon juice
1 cup oil, for frying

DIRECTIONS:

- In a bowl, combine salt, garlic, pepper, cumin powder, and cinnamon powder and toss. Set aside.
- Heat oil in the Instant Pot on sauté mode. Transfer the sweet potato into the oil and fry until golden.
- Place on a paper towel. Season with salt and pepper.
- Transfer to a serving dish, drizzle some lemon juice on top and serve.

37. Fried Mushrooms

(Time: 15 minutes \ Servings: 4)

INGREDIENTS:

2 oz. mushrooms, sliced
¼ teaspoon salt
¼ teaspoon black pepper

¼ garlic powder

4 tablespoons oil, for frying

DIRECTIONS:

- Heat oil the in Instant Pot on sauté mode. Fry mushrooms until golden.
- Transfer to a paper towel to drain excess oil. Season with garlic powder, salt and pepper. Drizzle lemon juice and enjoy.

38. Easy Cauliflower Hummus

(Time: 50 minutes \ Servings: 4)

INGREDIENTS:

2 cups cauliflower, chunks

1 pinch salt

¼ teaspoon chili powder

3 cups water

2 tablespoons olive oil

1 onion, chopped

2 garlic cloves, minced

DIRECTIONS:

- Transfer the water, cauliflower, salt, onion and garlic into the Instant Pot.
- Set it on slow mode.
- Cover with a lid and cook for 45 minutes.
- Let it cool a little then transfer into blender and blend to a puree.
- Add olive oil gradually and blend.
- Put to a serving dish and sprinkle chili powder on top.

39. Carrot Broccoli Stew

(Time: 55 minutes \ Servings: 3)

INGREDIENTS:

1 cup broccoli, florets

1 cup carrots, sliced

½ teaspoon salt

1 teaspoon black pepper

3 cups chicken broth

1 cup cream

DIRECTIONS:

- Add the broccoli florets, cream, carrots, salt, and chicken broth and toss well.
- Cook on stew mode for 40-45 minutes.
- Transfer into serving bowls and sprinkle black pepper on top.

40. Creamy Pumpkin Puree Soup

(Time: 55 minutes \ Servings: 3)

INGREDIENTS:

1 cup pumpkin puree
2 cups chicken broth
4-5 garlic cloves
salt and black pepper, to taste
1 cup cream
2 tablespoons olive oil

DIRECTIONS:

- In the Instant Pot, add all ingredients and cook on low heat for 40-45 minutes on stew mode.
- After that, transfer to a blender and blend well. Pour into a bowl and enjoy.

41. Instant Pot Creamy Mushrooms

(Time: 25 minutes \ Servings: 3)

INGREDIENTS:

1 cup mushrooms, sliced
1 cup cream
½ cup cream cheese
¼ teaspoon black pepper
½ teaspoon salt
2 garlic cloves, minced
2 tablespoons olive oil

DIRECTIONS:

- Set the Instant Pot on sauté mode and fry garlic for a minute.
- Add oil and sauté mushrooms for 4-5 minutes.
- Stir in the cream, chicken broth, and cream cheese and season with salt and pepper. Cook for 20-25 minutes on high pressure mode.

42. Stir Fried Garlic Zest Spinach

(Time: 25 minutes \ Servings: 3)

INGREDIENTS:

2 cups baby spinach
3-4 garlic cloves, thinly sliced
¼ teaspoon salt
½ cup chicken stock
4 tablespoons butter

DIRECTIONS:

- Set the Instant Pot on sauté mode, melt the butter and fry the garlic for 20 seconds.
- Add the spinach and stir fry for 10 minutes. Add in the chicken stock and mix well.
- When the water is dried out, season with salt and pepper.

43. Hot Stir-Fried Chili Pepper

(Time: 20 minutes \ Servings: 3)

INGREDIENTS:

2 green bell peppers, sliced
2 red bell peppers, fried
1 onion, sliced
½ teaspoon salt
½ teaspoon chili powder
½ teaspoon garlic paste
2 tablespoons olive oil

DIRECTIONS:

- In the Instant Pot, heat oil and fry the onion and the garlic. Add the salt, chili powder, and bell peppers and keep stirring. Stir fry for 10-15 minutes with few splashes of water. Transfer to a serving dish and serve.

44. Mango Mash with Sweet Potatoes

(Time: 35 minutes \ Servings: 3)

INGREDIENTS:

4 sweet potatoes, boiled, peeled
1 cup mango, chunks

1 cup sour cream
1 avocado, pulp
½ cup mango juice
¼ teaspoon salt
1 teaspoon black pepper
2 garlic cloves, minced
2 tablespoons olive oil

DIRECTIONS:

- Set the Instant Pot on slow mode.
- Add in the olive oil, avocado, cream, potatoes, salt, black pepper, mango juice and garlic and cover with a lid.
- Cook for 35 minutes.

45. Pineapple Lemonade Pilaf

(Time: 25 minutes \ Servings: 4)

INGREDIENTS:

1 cup cauliflower rice
1 cup pineapple juice
1 cup water
1 teaspoon salt
1 cup pineapple chunks
3 tablespoons lemon juice
½ teaspoon black pepper
1 onion, chopped
2 tablespoons cooking oil
a few pineapple slices
1 lime slice

DIRECTIONS:

- Set the Instant Pot on sauté mode.
- Heat oil and fry onion until softened.
- Add the pineapple juice, water, lemon juice, salt and pepper; then boil.
- Add in the cauliflower rice and boil on rice mode for 20 minutes.
- Garnish with pineapple and lime slices.

46. Spiced Zucchini Fingers

(Time: 15 minutes \ Servings: 5)

INGREDIENTS:

2 large zucchinis, sliced
1 teaspoon cumin powder
1 teaspoon cinnamon power
¼ teaspoon garlic powder
¼ teaspoon salt
2 tablespoons almond flour
½ teaspoon chili powder
½ cup cooking oil

DIRECTIONS:

- Roll out the zucchini slices into the flour and set aside.
- Set the Instant Pot on sauté mode.
- Heat oil and deep fry the zucchinis until lightly golden.
- Drain out the excessive oil on a piece of paper.
- Sprinkle with salt, chili powder, cinnamon powder, and cumin powder.

Fresh Veggies Snacks

47. Zucchini Chips
(Time: 15 minutes \ Servings: 4)

INGREDIENTS:

3 large zucchinis, thinly sliced
¼ teaspoon salt
¼ teaspoons black pepper
½ tablespoons cooking oil, for frying

DIRECTIONS:

- Heat oil in the Instant Pot on sauté mode.
- Put a few slices of zucchini in the Instant Pot and fry until golden and crisp.
- Repeat the same steps for all zucchini chips.
- Then place onto a paper towel to drain out the excessive oil. Season with salt and pepper.

48. Asparagus Chowder
(Time: 45 minutes \ Servings: 5)

INGREDIENTS:

1 tablespoon olive oil
2 cups chopped onion
2 teaspoons grated lemon rind
1 cup cauliflower rice
3 cans fat-free, chicken broth
2 cups sliced asparagus
2 cups chopped spinach
¼ teaspoons ground nutmeg
½ cup grated Parmesan cheese
½ teaspoon salt

DIRECTIONS:

- Heat oil in the Instant Pot. Add onion, stirring for 5 minutes until transparent.
- Now add the rice, lemon rind, asparagus, spinach, chicken broth, salt and cook for 10 minutes with covered lid. Turn off the heat and then top with parmesan

cheese and ground nutmeg.

49. Carrot and Pumpkin Stew

(Time: 60 minutes \ Servings: 4)

INGREDIENTS:

1 cup pumpkin, chopped
1 onion, chopped
4 carrots, peeled, chopped
1 teaspoon salt
1 teaspoon black pepper
½ teaspoon cumin powder
3-4 garlic cloves, minced
2 tablespoons olive oil
2 cups chicken broth
1 cup vegetable broth

DIRECTIONS:

- In the Instant Pot, add the pumpkin, carrots, chicken broth, onion, oil, salt, garlic, cumin powder, vegetable broth, and black pepper and mix well.
- Cover the pot with a lid and cook on slow mode for 60 minutes.
- Transfer to a blender and blend to a puree.
- Pour the stew into serving bowls and serve hot.

50. Tropic Cauliflower Manchurian

(Time: 35 minutes \ Servings: 4)

INGREDIENTS:

2 cups cauliflower florets
1 onion, chopped
1 teaspoon salt
1 teaspoon chili flakes
½ teaspoon cumin powder
3 green chilies, sliced
1 cup tomato puree
3 tablespoons tomato ketchup
½ teaspoon cinnamon powder
½ teaspoon garlic paste
¼ teaspoon turmeric powder

¼ cup cooking oil

DIRECTIONS:

- Heat oil in the Instant Pot on sauté mode.
- Add the cauliflower florets and fry until lightly golden, then set aside.
- In the same pot, sauté onion until transparent.
- Add in the tomato puree, tomato ketchup, salt, chili flakes, turmeric powder, and garlic paste and fry for 5-6 minutes.
- Add in the cauliflower and fry again for 4-5 minutes on high heat.
- Sprinkle cinnamon powder, cumin powder, and green chilies on top.

51. Garlic Fried Mushrooms

(Time: 15 minutes \ Servings: 3)

INGREDIENTS:

2 cups mushrooms, sliced
¼ teaspoon salt
1 teaspoon black pepper
½ teaspoon garlic paste
2 tablespoons soya sauce
1 teaspoon basil, chopped
2 tablespoons cooking oil

DIRECTIONS:

- Heat oil on sauté mode. Fry garlic for 30 seconds. Stir in the mushrooms and fry for 5-10 minutes on low heat. Add in the soya sauce and season with salt and pepper.
- Cook for 5 more minutes, stirring occasionally. Sprinkle basil on top and serve.

52. Tropic Sweet Potato Gravy

(Time: 25 minutes \ Servings: 4)

INGREDIENTS:

4 sweet potatoes, boiled, peeled, cut into cubes
1 onion, chopped
1 teaspoon cumin seeds
1 teaspoon chili powder
½ teaspoon cumin powder
1 cup tomato puree
½ teaspoon cinnamon powder

½ teaspoon garlic paste
½ teaspoon thyme
¼ teaspoon turmeric powder
2 tablespoons cooking oil
½ cup chicken broth

DIRECTIONS:

- Heat oil in the Instant Pot on sauté mode and sauté onion, cumin seeds and garlic for 1 minute.
- Add in the tomato puree, salt, chili powder, turmeric powder, and garlic paste and fry for 5-6 minutes.
- Add the potatoes and mix thoroughly.
- Stir in the chicken broth and cook for 10 minutes on medium heat.
- Sprinkle cinnamon powder, thyme and cumin powder on top.

53. Ground Beef Zucchini Zoodles

(Time: 35 minutes \ Servings: 4)

INGREDIENTS:

¼ lb. beef mince
1 large zucchini, spiralled
1 onion, chopped
2 tablespoons olive oil
2 tomatoes, chopped
2-3 garlic cloves, minced
½ teaspoon black pepper
¼ teaspoon chili powder
2 tablespoons soya sauce
1 oz. parmesan cheese, grated
¼ teaspoon salt

DIRECTIONS:

- Heat oil on sauté mode. Fry onion and garlic for a minute.
- Add the beef and fry until brown.
- Add in the tomatoes, salt, chili powder, soya sauce and black pepper.
- Transfer the fried ground beef to a bowl and set aside.
- In the same pot, add the zucchini zoodles and fry for 5-10 minutes.
- Add in the fried ground beef and mix well. Sprinkle cheese on top.

54. Stir Fried Vegetables

(Time: 15 minutes \ Servings: 4)

INGREDIENTS:

2 green bell peppers
1 yellow bell pepper
1 zucchini, sliced
1 onion, sliced
½ cup mushrooms, sliced
¼ teaspoon salt

¼ teaspoon chili powder
½ teaspoon garlic paste
2 tablespoons soya sauce
2 tablespoons vinegar
2 tablespoons oil

DIRECTIONS:

- Heat oil in the Instant Pot on sauté mode and stir fry all vegetables.
- Season with salt, pepper and soya sauce.
- Cover with a lid and cook for 5-10 minutes.

55. Eggplant and Sweet Potato Gravy

(Time: 55 minutes \ Servings: 5)

INGREDIENTS:

2 eggplants, sliced
2 sweet potatoes, peeled, diced
1 onion, chopped
3 large tomatoes, chopped
½ teaspoon salt
1 teaspoon chili powder
¼ teaspoon dry coriander powder
¼ teaspoon turmeric powder
½ teaspoon garlic paste
2 tablespoons cooking oil

DIRECTIONS:

- Heat oil in the Instant Pot on sauté mode and sauté onion until transparent.
- Add in the tomatoes, salt, chili powder, turmeric powder, and garlic paste and fry well. Add the eggplants and fry for 15 minutes on high heat.
- Add the potatoes, stirring continuously.
- Add a few splashes of water while frying. Cover with a lid and cook on low heat for 10-15 minutes. Sprinkle cumin powder and mix thoroughly.

Soups and Stews

56. Cauliflower Soup
(Time: 35 minutes \ Servings: 4)

INGREDIENTS:

- 1 cup cauliflower florets
- 1 teaspoon ginger paste
- 1 red bell pepper chopped
- 2 cups vegetable broth
- 2 tablespoons vinegar
- 1 lemon, sliced
- 1 green chili, chopped
- 4-5 garlic cloves, minced
- ½ teaspoon black pepper
- ¼ teaspoon salt
- 1 tablespoon oil

DIRECTIONS:

- Heat oil in the Instant Pot, add the ginger paste and cook for 1 minute on sauté mode.
- Add the cauliflower and fry well for 5-10 minutes.
- Add the bell pepper, salt, pepper, vinegar, green chilies, and lemon slices and mix well.
- Add the vegetable broth and cook on medium heat for 15 minutes on stew mode.
- Pour into serving bowls.

57. Green Beans and Spinach Soup
(Time: 15 minutes \ Servings: 4)

INGREDIENTS:

- 1 cup baby spinach
- 1 cup green beans
- 2 cups vegetable broth
- ½ cup full-fat milk
- 4-5 garlic cloves, minced
- 1 cup cream

½ cup tofu

    ½ teaspoon chili flakes

    ¼ teaspoon salt

    2 tablespoons oil

DIRECTIONS:

- Heat oil in the saucepan and add the garlic cloves, cook for 1 minute on sauté mode.
- Add the vegetable broth, spinach, green beans, tofu, cream, chili flake and salt, mix well.
- Cook on medium heat for 10 minutes on stew mode.
- Pour in the milk and cook for 5 minutes on low heat. Serve in bowls.

58. Coriander and Spinach Soup

(Time: 20 minutes \ Servings: 4)

INGREDIENTS:

    1 cup baby spinach

    1 bunch coriander, puree

    2 cups vegetable broth

    1 cup heavy cream

    ½ cup full-fat milk

    4-5 garlic cloves, minced

    ½ teaspoon chili flakes

    ¼ teaspoon salt

    2 tablespoons oil

DIRECTIONS:

- Heat oil in the saucepan and add garlic cloves, cook for 1 minute on sauté mode.
- Add vegetable broth, spinach, coriander puree, cream, chili flake, and salt, mix well.
- Cook on medium heat for 10 minutes on stew mode.
- Pour in milk and cook for 5 minutes on low heat.
- Spoon into serving bowls.

59. Shrimp Soup

(Time: 25 minutes \ Servings: 4)

INGREDIENTS:

2 oz. shrimp
2 cups chicken broth
¼ cup apple cider vinegar
4-5 garlic cloves, minced
½ teaspoon black pepper
¼ teaspoon salt
1 tablespoon oil
2 tomatoes, sliced

DIRECTIONS:

- Heat oil and add garlic cloves, fry for 1 minute. Add the shrimp and fry for 10 minutes.
- Season with salt and pepper.
- Add chicken broth, tomatoes, and vinegar and stir well.
- Cook on medium heat for 10 minutes on stew mode.
- Pour into serving bowls.

60. Pumpkin Soup

(Time: 16 minutes \ Servings: 3)

INGREDIENTS:

2 teaspoon olive oil
1 onion, chopped
1 carrot, chopped
2 cloves garlic, minced
2 tsp. curry powder
4 cups vegetable broth
2 teaspoon pumpkin seeds
salt to taste

DIRECTIONS:

- Add oil into the instant pot and let it sauté.
- Mix vegetable broth, pumpkin seeds, salt, curry powder, garlic, carrots and onion.
- Let it cook on high pressure for 10 minutes. When done, serve!

61. Mushroom Soup

(Time: 16 minutes \ Servings: 3)

INGREDIENTS:

2 teaspoon butter
1 onion, chopped
3 cups mushrooms, chopped
2 garlic cloves
2 cups thyme, chopped
2 teaspoon almond flour
3 cups chicken stock
2 cups parmesan cheese, shredded
salt to taste

DIRECTIONS:

-   Add butter and onion into the instant pot. Stir in mushrooms, garlic cloves, thyme, chicken stock and flour. Add salt. Let it cook on high pressure for 10 minutes.

-   When done, sprinkle shredded cheese on it and enjoy!

62. Chicken and Green Onion Soup

(Time: 14 minutes \ Servings: 3)

INGREDIENTS:

1 lb. chicken breast, shredded
2 cups chicken stock
1 teaspoon ginger
2 teaspoon sesame oil
salt to taste
green onions, chopped

DIRECTIONS:

-   Add sesame oil into the instant pot and let it sauté.
-   Mix in the chicken stock, chicken breast, ginger, salt and green onions.
-   Cook on high pressure for 10 minutes. When ready, serve!

63. Delicious Full Chicken Soup

(Time: 13 minutes \ Servings: 2)

INGREDIENTS:

2 lb. chicken breast fillet, strips
1 teaspoon canola oil
1 tsp. oregano powder
2 red bell peppers, sliced
2 green bell peppers, sliced
2 onions, sliced
4 slices provolone cheese
4 cups chicken broth
salt and pepper, to taste

DIRECTIONS:

- Add canola oil into the instant pot and cook chicken fillets.
- Mix in the oregano powder, salt and pepper, red bell pepper, green bell pepper and onion.
- Cook for 10 minutes. Add chicken broth. Cook for another 4 minutes. When done, serve and enjoy!

64. Baby Spinach Soup

(Time: 19 minutes \ Servings: 3)

INGREDIENTS:

2 teaspoon ginger, minced
4 garlic cloves, minced
1 teaspoon mustard seeds
1 teaspoon vegetable oil
2 cups vegetable broth
1 teaspoon coriander powder
1 teaspoon cumin powder
4 cups baby spinach

DIRECTIONS:

- Add oil into the instant pot and sauté it.
- Mix in the mustard seeds, garlic, cumin powder, coriander powder and vegetable broth.
- Add chopped spinach and cook for 15 minutes. When ready, serve.

65. Squash Soup

(Time: 15 minutes \ Servings: 3)

INGREDIENTS:

1 lb. squash
2 teaspoon butter
1 onion, chopped
2 garlic cloves, minced
3 cups chicken broth
2 teaspoon nutmeg powder
½ cup half and half
1 lb. chicken breast, cubed

DIRECTIONS:

- Add butter into the instant pot and sauté it. Mix squash, chicken broth, garlic, onion, nutmeg powder, chicken cubes and half and half. Cook for 10 minutes on high pressure.

66. Sweet and Sour Tomato Soup

(Time: 35 minutes \ Servings: 3)

INGREDIENTS:

1 cup tomato sauce
½ cup tomato ketchup
2 cups vegetable broth
¼ cup water
3 tablespoons of almond flour
2 tablespoons vinegar
2 garlic cloves, minced
½ teaspoon black pepper
¼ teaspoon salt
1 tablespoon oil

DIRECTIONS:

- Set the Instant Pot on sauté mode. Heat oil inside it and add garlic cloves, sauté for 1 minute. Add tomato puree, tomato ketchup, and vinegar and fry for 1-2 minutes. Stir in vegetable broth, and season with salt and pepper.
- Let it simmer for 20-25 minutes on stew mode.Combine water with almond flour and mix well.

- Gradually add this mixture into the soup and stir continuously for 1-2 minutes.
- Pour into serving bowls and enjoy.

67. Vegetable Soup

(Time: 30 minutes \ Servings: 3)

INGREDIENTS:

1 cup broccoli florets
1 green bell pepper, sliced
1 red bell pepper, sliced
1 carrot, sliced
1 onion, sliced
2 cups vegetable broth
1 tablespoon lemon juice
4-5 garlic cloves, minced
½ teaspoon black pepper
¼ teaspoon salt
1 tablespoon cooking oil

DIRECTIONS:

- Set the Instant Pot on sauté mode. Heat oil, add onion and garlic cloves, sauté for 1 minute.
- Add all vegetables, stir fry and cook on low heat for 5-10 minutes.
- Add vegetable broth, salt, and pepper and mix well. Cook on stew mode for 15 minutes.
- Drizzle lemon juice. Ladle into serving bowls and enjoy.

68. Garlic Chicken and Egg Soup

(Time: 35 minutes \ Servings: 3)

INGREDIENTS:

¼ lb. chicken, cut into small pieces
1 onion, chopped
2 eggs, whisked
2 cups chicken broth
¼ cup water
3 tablespoons of almond flour
4-5 garlic cloves, minced

½ teaspoon black pepper
¼ teaspoon salt
1 tablespoon oil

DIRECTIONS:

- Heat oil in the Instant Pot on sauté mode, sauté garlic and onion for 1 minute.
- Add the chicken and fry for 10 minutes. Shred chicken and transfer it to the Instant Pot again.
- Season with black pepper and salt. Add the chicken broth, simmer for 15 minutes on stew mode.
- In a bowl, combine water with almond flour and mix well.
- Gradually pour this mixture into soup and stir continuously for 2 minutes.
- Add the eggs by gradually. Cook for another 2 minutes. Ladle into bowls and enjoy.

69. Pumpkin Purée Soup

(Time: 35 minutes \ Servings: 3)

INGREDIENTS:

2 cups pumpkin puree
2 cups vegetable broth
1 cup full-fat milk
2 tablespoons soya sauce
¼ teaspoon turmeric powder
½ teaspoon black pepper
4-5 garlic cloves, minced
¼ teaspoon salt
1 tablespoon oil

DIRECTIONS:

- Heat oil in the Instant Pot and add garlic cloves, cook for 1 minute on sauté mode.
- Add pumpkin and fry for 5 minutes.
- Stir in vegetable broth, salt, pepper, turmeric powder, and soya sauce and mix, cook on low heat for 20 minutes on stew mode.Add milk and cook for another 5 minutes. Ladle the soup into serving bowls.

70. Spinach Soup

(Time: 35 minutes \ Servings: 3)

INGREDIENTS:

1 cup baby spinach
2 cups vegetable broth
½ cup full-fat milk
2 garlic cloves, minced
½ teaspoon chili flakes
¼ cup sour cream
2 tablespoons oil

DIRECTIONS:

- In the Instant Pot, add all ingredients and cover with a lid. Set the pot on stew mode, cook for 25 minutes. Transfer to a blender and blend until creamy.
- Pour the spinach soup back into the pot and cook for another 6 minutes. Top with sour cream.

71. Butter Squash Soup

(Time: 25 Minutes \ Servings: 6)

INGREDIENTS

1 peeled and diced butternut squash.
1 peeled and diced apple
1 teaspoon of ginger powder or pureed ginger
4 cups chicken broth
2 teaspoon of coconut oil to taste

DIRECTIONS

- Start by hitting the sauté button on the Instant Pot to pre¬heat it.
- When you can see the word "HOT", add the coconut oil and add some of the butternut squash cubes to it. Brown it lightly for approximately 5 minutes.
- Add the remaining squash and add the rest of the ingredients.
- Close and lock the Instant Pot. Press (+) button so 10 more minutes are added at high pressure.
- When the time is over, open the Instant Pot by using the Quick Release.
- Puree the mixture in a blender. Serve and enjoy the delicious, healthy soup.

72. Creamy Asparagus Soup

(Time: 20 Minutes \ Servings: 4)

INGREDIENTS

½ lb. of fresh asparagus, cut into pieces

1 sliced yellow onion

3 chopped or minced cloves of garlic cloves

3 teaspoon of coconuts oil

½ tsp. of dried thyme

5 cups bone broth

1 teaspoon lemon juice and zest

2 cups organic sour cream

DIRECTIONS

- Prepare the asparagus, onion, and garlic. Remove the woody ends from the asparagus stalks and discard it. Chop the asparagus into 1-inch pieces.
- Slice the onion into halves and chop it. Smash the garlic cloves or chop it. Then set the ingredients aside and place the stainless-steel bowl inside the Instant Pot without putting the lid on. Set to "Sauté" and add the coconut oil; then add the onions and the garlic.
- Cook the mixture for 5 minutes and stir occasionally; add the thyme and cook for 1 more minute. Add the broth, asparagus, and lemon zest with the salt. Then lock the lid of the Instant Pot and press the Manual button high pressure.
- Set the pressure timer to 5 minutes, and when the timer goes off, add the sour cream and stir after the Instant Pot releases the steam. Serve and enjoy.

73. Cauliflower Creamy Soup

(Time: 20 Minutes \ Servings: 5)

INGREDIENTS

4 cups vegetable broth

1 head of cubed and chopped cauliflower

3 cups chopped sweet potatoes

4 cups onion

2 large carrots

½ cup celery

2 teaspoon of raw coconut amino

1 teaspoon of coconut oil

DIRECTIONS

- Pour the coconut oil in the Instant Pot and add all ingredients inside.
- Lock the lid and seal the vent of the steam.
- Press the Manual button and adjust the timer to 9 minutes of cooking time.
- Once the pressure is reached, the countdown starts.
- Add 2 tsp. of cashew butter.
- Use a blender to mash the soup and add a few cups of kale for nutritional value.
- Garnish and serve.

74. Spinach Soup with Asparagus

(Time: 30 Minutes \ Servings: 5)

INGREDIENTS

2 courgettes
1 handful of kale
2 celery sticks
4 asparagus spears
¼ lb. of baby spinach
1 small onion
¼ quarter of deseeded chili
2 minced garlic cloves
2 teaspoon of coconut oil
1 pinch of salt
1 pinch of ground black pepper
1 cube of vegetable stock
2 tsp. of spirulina
½ cup fresh parsley

DIRECTIONS

- Start by peeling and chopping the onion, garlic, and chili and set it aside for 5 to 10 minutes. Finely chop the parsley and the vegetables.
- Add 2 teaspoon of oil into a preheated Instant Pot; then add the onion and press the Sauté button for 3 minutes. Once the onion softens, cancel the sauté. Add the garlic and chili.
- Add the chopped vegetables and leaves, except the parsley. Add the stock, salt, and pepper; then lock the lid and set the timer to 10 minutes.
- Once the timer goes off, release the pressure and blend the ingredients. Add the

spirulina and cook for 5 more minutes, then serve and enjoy the soup.

- Drain and rinse the noodles and add them to the Instant Pot.
- Let the ingredients simmer for around 2 minutes; then garnish with cilantro and enjoy!

75. Beef and Broccoli Stew

(Time: 35 Minutes \ Servings: 4-5)

INGREDIENTS

1 lb. of beef stew meat
1 large quartered onion
½ cup beef or bone broth
¼ cup coconut aminos
2 teaspoon of fish sauce
2 large minced cloves of garlic
1 tsp. of ground ginger
½ tsp. of salt
1 teaspoon of coconuts oil
¼ lb. of frozen broccoli

DIRECTIONS

- In the Instant Pot, place all ingredients except the broccoli. Lock the lid. Press the Meat/Stew button and cook for 35 minutes.
- When the timer goes off, carefully release the pressure and open the lid. Add the broccoli to the inner pot. Place the lid loosely.
- Let the ingredients simmer for around 15 minutes. Serve and enjoy the stew.

Chicken Recipes

76. Chicken Wings

(Time: 35 minutes \ Servings: 5)

INGREDIENTS:

3 chicken breasts, cut into 2 inch pieces
1 teaspoon garlic powder
1 cup almond flour
2 tablespoons coriander, chopped
½ teaspoon salt
½ teaspoon chili pepper
½ teaspoon cinnamon powder
1 cup oil, for frying
¼ cup water

DIRECTIONS:

- In a bowl, combine flour, salt, chili powder, cumin powder, coriander and toss well.
- Add water and make a thick paste.
- Heat oil in the Instant Pot on sauté mode.
- Dip each chicken piece into the flour mixture and then put into the oil.
- Fry each chicken wing until golden and place on a paper towel to drain out the excessive oil.
- Transfer to a serving dish and serve with mint sauce.
- Enjoy.

77. Whole Chicken

(Time: 70 minutes \ Servings: 6)

INGREDIENTS:

1 white chicken
1 teaspoon garlic paste
1 teaspoon ginger paste
1 teaspoon salt
1 teaspoon cayenne pepper
¼ teaspoon chili powder

½ teaspoon black pepper

½ teaspoon cinnamon powder

½ teaspoon cumin powder

3 tablespoons lemon juice

2 tablespoons apple cider vinegar

2 tablespoons soya sauce

3 tablespoons olive oil

DIRECTIONS:

- In a bowl, combine vinegar, cayenne pepper, lemon juice, ginger garlic paste, salt, pepper, chili powder, olive oil, cumin powder and cinnamon powder, mix well.
- Pour over the chicken and rub with all over hands.
- Put the chicken in a greased Instant Pot and cover up with a lid.
- Cook on slow mode for 65-70 minutes.

78. Broccoli Chicken

(Time: 45 minutes \ Servings: 3)

INGREDIENTS:

¼ lb. chicken, boneless, cut into small pieces

1 cup broccoli florets

2-3 garlic cloves garlic, minced

1 teaspoon salt

½ teaspoon black pepper

3 tablespoons butter

1 cup chicken broth

2 cup cream

DIRECTIONS:

- Melt butter in the Instant Pot on sauté mode and fry garlic for 1 minute.
- Add the chicken and stir fry until golden Season with salt and pepper.
- Add broccoli and cream and pour in the chicken broth.
- Cook on manual mode for 10 minutes.

79. Simple Chicken Wings

(Time: 20 minutes \ Servings: 4)

INGREDIENTS:

 2 lb. chicken wings –
 1 cup BBQ sauce –

DIRECTIONS:

- Put the chicken wings in the instant pot and cover them with the BBQ sauce.
- Cover the lid and cook on high pressure for 20 minutes.
- When ready, serve and enjoy the delicious wings.

80. Delicious Chicken

(Time: 15 minutes \ Servings: 3)

INGREDIENTS:

 2 cups chicken broth
 2 chicken breasts, diced
 4 green chilies, chopped
 1 onion, chopped
 4 sweet potatoes, diced
 1 bell pepper, sliced
 2 garlic cloves minced
 ½ teaspoon cumin powder
 ½ cup tomato sauce
 Taco seasoning
 Salt to taste

DIRECTIONS:

- Add chicken broth into the instant pot and cook for 5 minutes.
- Mix in the green chilies, onion, potatoes, garlic cloves, bell pepper and salt.
- Add cumin powder with chicken breasts and cook for 10 minutes.
- Mix in the tomato sauce and stir well. When ready, serve with the taco seasoning and enjoy!

81. Asian-Style Chicken Thighs

(Time: 20 minutes \ Servings: 4)

INGREDIENTS:

1 teaspoon vegetable oil
1 lb. chicken thighs
1 onion , chopped
2 teaspoon ginger, minced
2 teaspoon garlic, mince
2 ½ cups chicken broth
½ cup ketchup
2 teaspoon wine vinegar

DIRECTIONS:

- Add vegetable oil into the instant pot with ginger and garlic. Hit the sauté button and when it beeps.

- Add the chicken thighs. Let it cook for 10 minutes. Add onion and chicken broth.

- Let it cook for 10 minutes on pressure. Meanwhile, mix ketchup, mirin and wine vinegar in a bowl.

- Serve the chicken with this sauce and enjoy!

82. Chicken Breast with Green Onions

(Time: 25 minutes \ Servings: 4)

INGREDIENTS:

4 chicken breast, diced
½ teaspoon soy sauce
2 cups water
½ teaspoon stevia
2 teaspoon wine vinegar
1 teaspoon sesame oil
2 teaspoon chili garlic sauce
1 teaspoon flaxseed meal
2 green onions, chopped
½ teaspoon red pepper flakes

DIRECTIONS:

- Add water, soy sauce and wine vinegar into the instant pot. Let it cook for 10 minutes.
- Add the chicken pieces. Mix well.
- Add sesame oil, chili garlic sauce, green onions, red pepper flakes and flaxseed meal.
- Let it cook on pressure for 10 minutes.
- When it beeps, take it out and enjoy the saucy chicken.

83. Chicken with Sesame oil

(Time: 20 minutes \ Servings: 3)

INGREDIENTS:

1 teaspoon flaxseed meal
2 egg whites
1 lb. chicken, sliced
1 teaspoon soy sauce
1 teaspoon sesame oil
1 teaspoon wine vinegar
1 teaspoon ginger, grated
2 teaspoon garlic cloves, minced
salt and pepper, to taste

DIRECTIONS:

- Mix flaxseed meal and egg whites in a bowl.
- Add the mixture into the instant pot.
- Mix in the chicken, soy sauce, sesame oil, wine vinegar, ginger, garlic, and salt and pepper.
- Cook for 20 minutes on high pressure.
- When ready, serve!

84. Chicken Mushroom Mix

(Time: 14 minutes \ Servings: 2)

INGREDIENTS:

3 cups chicken, shredded
1 teaspoon oil

1 onion, chopped
6 small mushrooms, chopped
2 minced garlic cloves
1 cup spinach
½ cup parsley, chopped
2 cups full-fat milk
Salt and pepper, to taste
Almonds for seasoning

DIRECTIONS:

- Place chicken into a bowl. Mix in the onion, mushrooms, garlic, spinach and parsley. Blend well. Add milk and salt and pepper.
- Get a round baking tray.
- Grease it with oil. Add the mixture.
- Cook it in the instant pot for 10 minutes on high pressure.
- When ready, serve with almond seasoning!

85. Chicken Tenders with Garlic

(Time: 13 minutes \ Servings: 2)

INGREDIENTS:

1 lb. chicken tenders
2 garlic cloves, minced
2 teaspoon paprika
2 teaspoon oregano powder
2 teaspoon oil
1 onion, chopped
2 cups green beans, frozen
1 cup almond flour
1 cup chicken stock
1 Egg, raw
Salt and pepper, to taste

DIRECTIONS:

- Add oil into the instant pot.
- Mix in the chicken tenders, garlic, paprika, oregano, onion, green beans, flour and chicken stock.
- Add egg with salt and pepper. Cook for 10 minutes on high pressure.

86. Hot Chicken Chili

(Time: 25 minutes \ Servings: 3)

INGREDIENTS:

2 chicken breasts
1 cup chili garlic sauce
¼ cup tomato ketchup
4 tablespoons stevia
2 tablespoons soya sauce
2 tomatoes, chopped
¼ teaspoon salt
¼ teaspoon cayenne pepper
3 tablespoons olive oil

DIRECTIONS:

- Combine the chili garlic sauce, tomato ketchup, soya sauce, stevia, salt, and pepper and mix.
- Pour the sauce over the chicken and toss well.
- Heat oil in the Instant Pot on sauté mode and add in the chicken breasts.
- Cover and cook on pressure cook mode for 20 minutes. Transfer to a serving dish and serve.

87. Hot Garlic Chicken Breasts

(Time: 35 minutes \ Servings: 5)

INGREDIENTS:

2 chicken breasts
2 tablespoons apple cider vinegar
1 cup tomato ketchup
1 teaspoon garlic powder
¼ teaspoon salt
½ teaspoon chili powder
3 tablespoons olive oil

DIRECTIONS:

- Combine the vinegar, ketchup, chili powder, salt, and garlic powder.
- Drizzle over the chicken and toss well. Set the Instant Pot on sauté mode and heat oil. Transfer the chicken breasts in the pot. Cook for 35 minutes.

88. Fried Chicken Mince

(Time: 35 minutes \ Servings: 4)

INGREDIENTS:

1 cup ground chicken
1 onion, chopped
2-3 garlic cloves, minced
¼ teaspoon cumin powder
¼ teaspoon cinnamon powder
2 tomatoes, chopped
1 teaspoon salt
½ teaspoon black pepper
2 tablespoons olive oil

DIRECTIONS:

- Heat oil in the Instant Pot on sauté mode and fry garlic and onion for 1 minute.
- Add the ground chicken and stir fry until its color changes. Season with salt and pepper.
- Stir in the tomatoes and sauté for 3-4 minutes. Cook for 5-8 minutes, then turn off the heat.
- Sprinkle cumin powder and cinnamon powder. Serve hot.

89. Chicken and Turnip Stew

(Time: 45 minutes \ Servings: 7)

INGREDIENTS:

1 onion, chopped
2 tomatoes, chopped
1 cup chicken pieces
2-3 turnips, peeled, diced
2 cups chicken broth
1 carrot, sliced
1 tablespoon coriander, chopped
½ teaspoon garlic paste
½ teaspoon ginger paste
½ teaspoon cumin powder
½ teaspoon cinnamon power
½ teaspoon chili powder

¼ teaspoon salt
¼ teaspoon turmeric powder
3 tablespoons oil
2 green chilies, whole

DIRECTIONS:

- Heat oil, sauté onion for 1 minute on sauté mode.
- Stir in the tomatoes, ginger garlic paste, salt, chili powder, and turmeric powder and fry for 1 minute.
- Add the chicken pieces and cook until lightly golden. Add the turnips and fry with chicken until tender.
- Now add the chicken broth, coriander, carrots, and green chili and cook on low heat for 30 minutes on stew mode. Add cinnamon and cumin powder and stir.

90. Hot Butter Chicken

(Time: 40 minutes \ Servings: 4)

INGREDIENTS:

¼ lb. chicken, boneless, pieces
1 cup tomato puree
1-inch ginger slice
1-2 red chilies
½ teaspoon garlic paste
1 teaspoon salt
¼ teaspoon black pepper
4 tablespoons butter

DIRECTIONS:

- In a blender, add tomato puree, chilies, ginger, garlic, salt, and pepper and blend well.
- Melt butter in the Instant Pot on sauté mode and fry the chicken for 5-10 minute.
- Transfer the tomato mixture and combine.
- Cook on low heat for 10-15 minutes until the chicken tenders. Transfer to a serving dish and enjoy.

91. Tropic Shredded Chicken

(Time: 30 minutes \ Servings: 4)

INGREDIENTS:

3 chicken breasts, shredded, boiled
½ teaspoon garlic paste
½ teaspoon salt
½ teaspoon soya sauce
2 tablespoons barbecue sauce
½ teaspoon chili powder
2 tablespoons oil

DIRECTIONS:

- Heat oil in the Instant Pot on sauté mode and fry garlic for 1 minute.
- Add the chicken breasts and fry until lightly golden.
- Add soya sauce, barbecue sauce, salt, and chili powder and fry well.
- Place into a serving dish and enjoy.

92. Chicken with Avocado Cream

(Time: 35 minutes \ Servings: 6)

INGREDIENTS

4 lb. of organic chicken
1 teaspoon of coconut oil
1 tsp. of paprika
1 ½ cups Pacific Chicken Bone Broth
1 tsp. of dried thyme
¼ tsp. of freshly ground black pepper
1 tsp. of ginger
2 teaspoon of lemon juice
½ tsp. of sea salt
6 cloves of peeled garlic
1 Avocado

DIRECTIONS

- In a medium bowl, combine the paprika, thyme, salt, dried ginger, and pepper. Then rub the seasoning over the outer parts of the chicken.
- Heat the oil in the Instant Pot and let it simmer. Add the chicken breast side down and cook it for 6 minutes.

- Now, flip the chicken and add the broth, lemon juice, and garlic cloves. Lock the lid and set the timer to 30 minutes on High pressure.
- Prepare the avocado cream by whisking the contents of the avocado with 2 teaspoon of coconut oil and ½ tsp. of salt. Once the timer beeps, naturally release the pressure.
- Remove the chicken from the Instant Pot and set it aside for 5 minutes before serving it. Enjoy the meal.

93. Chicken with Sweet Potatoes

(Time: 30 minutes \ Servings: 4)

INGREDIENTS

2 cups cubed and peeled sweet potatoes
2 teaspoon of coconut oil
1 lb. of skinless and boneless cubed chicken breast halves
3 minced cloves of garlic
6 teaspoon of tamari soy sauce
1 cup water
3 teaspoon of stevia
3 teaspoon of hot sauce
1 peeled and diced mango
¼ tsp. of smashed red pepper flakes
1 tsp. of flaxseed meal
1 tsp. of ginger
1 cup warm water

DIRECTIONS

- Start by placing the sweet potatoes in the Instant Pot and pour enough water so the potatoes are covered. Press manual and set the timer to 10 minutes on High pressure.
- Seal the lid, and when the timer goes off, quickly release the pressure and drain the potatoes.
- Place 2 teaspoon of coconut oil in the Instant Pot and add the chicken. Sauté for 5 minutes. Sprinkle the ginger and garlic and cook for several more minutes. Add the tamari, a cup of warm water, and the stevia with the hot sauce.
- Add the flaxseed meal to the mixture and set on Boil feature for 10 minutes. Serve and enjoy the healthy chicken lunch with sweet potatoes.

94. Egg and Carrot Spread
(Time: 25 minutes \ Servings: 3)

INGREDIENTS:

4 eggs, whisked
3 carrots, shredded, boiled
¼ teaspoons slat
½ teaspoon black pepper
3 tablespoons butter

DIRECTIONS:

- In a blender, add the carrots and blend them to a puree.
- Add them to the Instant Pot and let simmer for 2 minutes.
- Add the eggs, butter, salt, and pepper, stir continually for 10-15 minutes.
- Cook for 5 minutes on low heat.
- Serve hot and enjoy.

95. Egg and Carrots Crumb
(Time: 25 minutes \ Servings: 3)

INGREDIENTS:

4 eggs
1 carrot, shredded
1 pinch of salt
½ teaspoon black pepper
3 tablespoons butter

DIRECTIONS:

- Melt butter on sauté mode.
- Sauté carrots for 5-10 minutes until the water evaporates.
- Add the eggs, salt and pepper, stir continuously.
- Cook for 5 minutes.

96. Bell Pepper and Egg Tortilla
(Time: 25 minutes \ Servings: 3)

INGREDIENTS:

4 eggs, whisked

1 red bell pepper, chopped
1 onion, chopped
¼ teaspoons slat
½ teaspoon black pepper
3 tablespoons butter

DIRECTIONS:

- In a bowl, add the eggs, onion, bell peppers, salt, and pepper, mix well.
- Melt butter in the pot on sauté mode.
- Pour the eggs mixture and spread all over and cover the pot with a lid.
- Cook for 15 minutes on manual mode.
- Serve hot and enjoy.

97. Roasted Eggs Gravy

(Time: 30 minutes \ Servings: 4)

INGREDIENTS:

4 eggs
1 onion, chopped
2 tomatoes, chopped
¼ teaspoon pinch salt
½ teaspoon chili powder
¼ teaspoon turmeric powder
1/3 teaspoon cumin powder
1-2 garlic cloves, minced
2 tablespoons olive oil

DIRECTIONS:

- Heat oil in the Instant Pot on sauté mode and fry the eggs until lightly golden. Set aside.
- In the same oil, fry onion until lightly golden.
- Add tomatoes, garlic, salt, chili powder, and turmeric powder and fry until the tomatoes soften.
- Now transfer to a blender and blend well.
- Return the mixture to the pot again and fry with a few splashes of water.
- Add in the roasted eggs and toss around.

98. Squash with Eggs

(Time: 30 minutes \ Servings: 4)

INGREDIENTS:

4 eggs
1 squash, cut into 1-inch thick rings
1 pinch salt
1 pinch chili powder
2 tablespoons olive oil

DIRECTIONS:

- Spray the Instant Pot with oil.
- Place the squash rings in the Instant Pot and crack an egg into each ring.
- Sprinkle with salt and pepper.
- Cover with a lid and cook for 25 minutes on pressure cook mode.

99. Tomato Eggs

(Time: 10 minutes \ Servings: 2)

INGREDIENTS:

2 eggs, whisked
2 tomatoes, sliced
1 teaspoon garlic powder
¼ teaspoon salt
½ teaspoon chili powder
3 tablespoons butter

DIRECTIONS:

- Melt butter on sauté mode. Add the eggs and spread all over.
- Cook for 1-2 minutes then flip.
- Place the tomato slices and in the Instant Pot and cover the pot with a lid.
- Cook on high pressure cook mode for 10 minutes.
- Season with salt and chili powder.

100.   Zucchini Egg

(Time: 15 minutes \ Servings: 2)

INGREDIENTS:

2 eggs, whisked
1 large zucchini, sliced
1 teaspoon garlic powder
¼ teaspoon salt
¼ teaspoon black pepper
3 tablespoons butter

DIRECTIONS:

- Melt butter in the Instant Pot on sauté mode. Fry zucchini for 3-4 minutes.
- Pour the eggs mixture and spread evenly.
- Cook for 2-3 minutes on one side then flip over.
- Season with salt and pepper.

101.   Peperoni Pizza Egg

(Time: 15 minutes \ Servings: 2)

INGREDIENTS:

2 eggs, whisked
1 teaspoon garlic powder
¼ teaspoon salt
½ teaspoon black pepper
1 onion, chopped
4-5 pepperoni slices
3 tablespoons butter

DIRECTIONS:

- In the whisked eggs, add in the onion, and pepperoni, season with salt, garlic and pepper.
- Melt butter in the Instant Pot on sauté mode.
- Pour the eggs mixture and stir continuously.
- Cook for 1-2 minutes and then transfer to a serving platter.

102.   Poached Eggs

(Time: 10 minutes \ Servings: 3)

INGREDIENTS:

3 eggs
3 cups water
2 tablespoons vinegar
1 pinch salt

DIRECTIONS:

- Set the Instant Pot on pressure cook mode. Add water and let it boil.
- Crack 1 egg into a bowl and pour it in the boiled water. Repeat for all eggs. Cover with a lid and cook for 5 minutes. Ladle to a serving platter and enjoy.

103.   Asian Style Steamed Eggs

(Time: 10 Minutes \ Servings: 2)

INGREDIENTS

2 large eggs
⬚ cup cold water
2 stem of scallions, chopped
1 pinch of sesame seeds
1 pinch of fine garlic powder
pinch of salt and black pepper

1 pinch of flax seeds powder
2 avocados
1 tsp. of ginger
1 tsp. of flax seed powder
1 teaspoon of coconut oil

DIRECTIONS

- Start by placing the eggs into the water in a small bowl.
- Strain the eggs mixture above a mesh strainer above a heat proof bowl.
- Now, add what is left of the ingredients, except for the avocados.
- Mix very well and set aside. Pour water in the inner pot of the Instant Pot and place the trivet or the steamer basket. Place the bowl with the above mixture inside the trivet or the steamer basket.
- Seal the lid of the Instant Pot tightly and make sure to close the vent valve. Now, press the button "Manual" and set the heat to HIGH.
- Set the timer to 5 minutes.
- And when you hear the beep, open the lid and serve the eggs with cooked quinoa and the avocado.

Red Meat

---

104.   Pork Steaks
(Time: 65 minutes \ Servings: 5)

INGREDIENTS:

2 pork fillets
1 teaspoon garlic powder
½ teaspoon chili powder
2 tablespoons soya sauce
4 tablespoons barbecue sauce
¼ teaspoon turmeric powder
1 teaspoon salt
2 tablespoons vinegar
4 tablespoons olive oil

DIRECTIONS:

- In a bowl, add vinegar, soya sauce, barbecue sauce, chili powder, salt, garlic powder and oil.
- Transfer to the Instant Pot and cook on pressure cook mode for 60 minutes.

105.   Mutton Gravy
(Time: 45 minutes \ Servings: 4)

INGREDIENTS:

½ lb mutton, boiled
1 cup tomato puree
1-inch ginger slice
½ teaspoon garlic paste
1 teaspoon salt
¼ teaspoon chili powder
1 cup water
½ teaspoon cumin powder
4 tablespoons oil

DIRECTIONS:

- Heat oil in the Instant Pot on sauté mode and fry tomatoes with chili powder, ginger, garlic and salt, for 5-10 minute. Add mutton and fry well.

- Add in water and cook on stew mode for 15-20 minutes. Sprinkle cumin powder and transfer to a serving dish.

106.   Beef with Green Beans

(Time: 17 minutes \ Servings: 2)

INGREDIENTS:

1 lb. ground beef
1 teaspoon lemon juice
2 teaspoon butter
2 cups green beans, frozen
1 onion, chopped
2 garlic cloves, minced
salt and pepper, to taste

DIRECTIONS:

- Add garlic into the instant pot.
- Mix in the lemon juice, butter, onion, beef with salt and pepper.
- Add green beans.
- Cook for 15 minutes on high pressure.
- When ready, serve and enjoy!

107.   Diced Meat with Sweet Potatoes

(Time: 22 minutes \ Servings: 3)

INGREDIENTS:

2 teaspoon oil
2 teaspoon soy sauce
1 lb. meat , diced
2 garlic cloves, minced
2 jalapeno peppers, chopped
2 cups sweet potatoes diced
1 cup broth, any
salt and pepper, to taste
cilantro and peanuts for garnishing

DIRECTIONS:

- Add oil into the instant pot.

- Mix in the soy sauce, meat, garlic, jalapeno peppers and potatoes.
- Add broth with salt and pepper.
- Cook for 20 minutes on high pressure.
- When ready, serve with cilantro and peanuts dressing.

108.   Simple Meatballs Recipe

(Time: 17 minutes \ Servings: 3)

INGREDIENTS:

1 lb. beef
½ onion, diced
1 carrot, diced
2 sticks celery, diced
3 garlic cloves, minced
1 cup marsala wine
2 cups beef broth
2 tomatoes, diced
½ teaspoon tomato paste
salt and pepper, to taste

DIRECTIONS:

- Select the option for browning on the instant pot and add carrot, onion, and celery.
- Remove from pot and keep it aside in a bowl.
- Now add garlic, Marsala wine, tomatoes, beef, and salt and pepper into the bowl.
- Mix well and make small balls out of it.
- Add beef broth and tomato paste into the instant pot.
- Place the meat balls in the pot.
- Let it cook for 10 minutes on high pressure.
- When ready, serve!

109.   Sweet Potatoes with Meat

(Time: 24 minutes \ Servings: 4)

INGREDIENTS:

2 teaspoon olive oil
2 sweet potatoes, diced

2 onion, diced
2 carrots, diced
1 lb. red meat, in chunks
3 garlic cloves, minced
1 teaspoon chili powder
1 teaspoon chipotle powder
1 tsp. cumin powder
2 tomatoes , diced
2 teaspoon lime juice
salt to taste

DIRECTIONS:

- Add oil into the instant pot and select the option for sauté.
- When it heats up lightly, add onion, garlic cloves, lime juice and red meat. Let it cook for 10 minutes.
- Now add chili powder, carrots, cumin powder, chipotle powder and salt.
- Add sweet potatoes and let it cook for 10 more minutes.
- When it beeps, take it out and serve.

110.   Diced Meat with Onions

(Time: 15 minutes \ Servings: 2)

INGREDIENTS:

1 large onion, sliced
1 teaspoon olive oil
1 lb. red meat , diced
2 tomatoes, chopped
½ teaspoon chili powder
salt and pepper, to taste

DIRECTIONS:

- Add onion and olive oil into the instant pot and press the sauté button.
- Mix in the tomatoes, red meat, chili powder, and salt and pepper.
- Let it cook for 10 minutes. When ready, serve with your favorite side dish!

111.   Sliced Meat Mixed Mushrooms
(Time: 13 minutes \ Servings: 3)

INGREDIENTS:

1 lb. beef meat, sliced
2 teaspoon onion powder
1 cup tomato paste
½ cup thyme, chopped
½ cup cheese, shredded
3 cups mushrooms, chopped
½ large onion, chopped
parsley to garnish

DIRECTIONS:

- Mix tomato paste with onion powder in a bowl.
- Put the tomato paste mixture in the instant pot and then add meat.
- Cover the meat with thyme, mushrooms and cheese. Cook it for 10 minutes.
- When ready, garnish it with chopped parsley and enjoy!

112.   Meat with Peppers
(Time: 15 minutes \ Servings: 2)

INGREDIENTS:

1 teaspoon vegetable oil
½ cup tomato sauce
1 lb. ground meat
2 green peppers, sliced
2 red peppers, sliced
1 onion , chopped
2 garlic cloves, chopped
½ teaspoon chili powder
salt and pepper, to taste

DIRECTIONS:

- Add garlic, onion and vegetable oil into the instant pot. Press the sauté button.
- Mix in the ground meat, green peppers and red peppers.
- Sprinkle salt, pepper and chili powder on the meat. Let it cook for 15 minutes.
- When ready, serve and enjoy!

113.   Meat with Onion Sauce

(Time: 16 minutes \ Servings: 2)

INGREDIENTS:

1 lb. meat steaks
2 cups meat broth
2 cloves garlic, chopped
2 cups vegetable broth
1 cup tomato paste
salt and pepper, to taste
1 Bay leaf
parsley, chopped to garnish

DIRECTIONS:

- Add vegetable broth into the instant pot and let it cook for 2 minutes.
- Mix in the meat broth, bay leaf, salt and pepper, meat steak, garlic and onion.
- Let it cook for 10 minutes. Release the pressure when the pot beeps.
- Take it out and garnish with parsley. Serve and enjoy!

114.   Carrot and Pork Stew

(Time: 45 minutes \ Servings: 7)

INGREDIENTS:

1 onion, chopped
2 tomatoes, chopped
2 carrots, sliced
½ lb. pork meat, pieces, boiled
2 cups chicken broth
½ teaspoon garlic paste
½ teaspoon ginger paste
½ teaspoon cumin powder
½ teaspoon cinnamon powder
½ teaspoon chili powder
¼ teaspoon salt
¼ teaspoon turmeric powder
3 tablespoons oil
2 green chilies, whole

DIRECTIONS:

- Heat oil in the Instant Pot, sauté onion for 1 minute on sauté mode.
- Stir in tomatoes, ginger paste, garlic paste, salt, chili powder, and turmeric powder and fry for 1 minute.
- Now add the pork, and fry for about 10 minutes.
- Add carrots and fry with them with the meat until lightly tender.
- Now add the chicken broth and green chili and cook on low heat for 30 minutes on stew mode.
- Add cinnamon and cumin powder and stir. Transfer to a serving dish and enjoy.

115. Hot Shredded Pork

(Time: 30 minutes \ Servings: 4)

INGREDIENTS:

2 pork fillets, boiled, shredded
½ teaspoon garlic paste
½ teaspoon salt
½ teaspoon soya sauce
2 tablespoons lemon juice
2 tablespoons barbecue sauce
½ cup chili garlic sauce
2 tablespoons vinegar
½ teaspoon chili powder
2 tablespoons oil

DIRECTIONS:

- Heat oil on sauté mode and fry garlic for 1 minute.
- Place the pork and fry well.
- Add soya sauce, chili garlic sauce, vinegar, barbecue sauce, salt, and chili powder and fry well.
- Transfer to a serving dish and drizzle lemon juice.

116. Mutton and Tomato Stew

(Time: 55 minutes \ Servings: 4)

INGREDIENTS:

1 cup tomato puree
1 cup mutton, pieces, boiled
2 tablespoons chili garlic sauce
2 cups chicken broth
1 garlic clove minced
1 red chili
¼ teaspoon salt
¼ teaspoon black pepper
2 tablespoons cooking oil

DIRECTIONS:

- In the Instant Pot, add the tomato puree, mutton, chicken broth, salt, pepper, garlic, chili, chili garlic sauce, and oil and stir well. Cover with a lid and cook on stew mode for 40 minutes.
- Transfer the soup to a blender and blend to a puree.
- Transfer back to the pot and let it simmer for 5 minutes.
- Pour to a serving dish and enjoy.

117. Pork Chops Gravy

(Time: 55 minutes \ Servings: 5)

INGREDIENTS:

½ lb. pork chops
1 onion, chopped
2-3 garlic cloves, minced
2 tomatoes, chopped
¼ teaspoon turmeric powder
¼ teaspoon cumin powder
¼ teaspoon cinnamon powder
1 teaspoon salt
½ teaspoon chili powder
4 tablespoons olive oil
½ cup chicken broth
1 green chili

DIRECTIONS:

- Heat oil on sauté mode and fry onion for 1 minute.
- Add in the tomatoes, chili powder, salt, and turmeric powder and fry.
- Now add the pork chops and stir fry for 5-10 minutes on high heat.
- Add the chicken broth on and cook on manual mode for 10-15 minutes.
- Sprinkle cumin powder and cinnamon powder, toss well. Place to a serving dish and enjoy.

118.   Mutton Broth

(Time: 60 minutes \ Servings: 4)

INGREDIENTS:

½ lb. mutton, pieces
3-4 garlic cloves
1 teaspoon salt
¼ teaspoon black pepper
½ teaspoon chili powder
1 onion, sliced
1-inch ginger slice
5 cups water
¼ teaspoon turmeric powder
¼ teaspoon dry coriander powder
1 cinnamon stick
3 tablespoons oil

DIRECTIONS:

- In the Instant Pot, add all ingredients and cook on slow mode for 2 hours.
- Stir occasionally.

119.   Mutton and Yogurt

(Time: 35 minutes \ Servings: 5)

INGREDIENTS:

½ lb. mutton, boiled
1 cup yogurt
1 onion, chopped
2-3 garlic cloves, minced
2 tomatoes, chopped

¼ teaspoon turmeric powder
¼ teaspoon cumin powder
¼ teaspoon cinnamon powder
1 teaspoon salt
½ teaspoon chili powder
4 tablespoons olive oil
½ cup chicken broth
1 green chili

DIRECTIONS:

- Heat oil in the Instant Pot on sauté mode and fry onion for 1 minute.
- Add in the tomatoes, chili powder, salt, and turmeric powder and fry.
- Add the mutton pieces and stir fry for 5-10 minutes on high heat.
- Stir in yogurt and fry until the oil disappears from the sides of the pan.
- Then add the chicken broth on and cook on manual mode for 10-15 minutes.
- Sprinkle cumin powder and cinnamon powder, toss well. Transfer to a serving dish and serve.

120.   Beef Okra

(Time: 35 minutes \ Servings: 4)

INGREDIENTS:

½ lb. mutton, boiled
1 cup okra
1 onion, chopped
2-3 garlic cloves, minced
2 tomatoes, chopped
¼ teaspoon turmeric powder
1 teaspoon salt
½ teaspoon chili powder
4 tablespoons olive oil

DIRECTIONS:

- Heat oil in the Instant Pot and fry the okra until crispy; then set aside.
- In the same pot, fry onion for 1 minute.
- Add in the tomatoes, chili powder, salt, turmeric powder and fry.
- Now add the mutton and stir fry for 5-10 minutes on high heat.
- Then add the okra and mix well. Transfer to a serving dish.

121. Beef and Sweet Potato Stew

(Time: 45 minutes \ Servings: 7)

INGREDIENTS:

1 onion, chopped
2 tomatoes, chopped
½ lb. beef, pieces, boiled
4 sweet potatoes, peeled, diced
2 cups chicken broth
½ teaspoon garlic paste
½ teaspoon ginger paste
½ teaspoon cumin powder
½ teaspoon cinnamon power
½ teaspoon chili powder
¼ teaspoon salt
¼ teaspoon turmeric powder
3 tablespoons oil
2 green chilies, whole

DIRECTIONS:

- Heat oil in the Instant Pot, sauté onion for 1 minute on sauté mode.
- Stir in tomatoes, ginger paste, garlic paste, salt, chili powder, and turmeric powder and fry for 1 minute.
- Now add the beef and fry for 10-11 minutes. Add potatoes and fry the beef until slightly tender.
- Now add the chicken broth, and green chili, and cook on low heat for 30 minutes on stew mode.
- Add cinnamon and cumin powder and stir.

122. Hot and Spicy Beef Gravy

(Time: 40 minutes \ Servings: 4)

INGREDIENTS:

½ lb. beef meat, cut into small pieces, boneless
1 cup tomato puree
1 onion, chopped
¼ garlic paste
1 teaspoon salt

½ teaspoon chili powder
½ teaspoon cumin powder
½ teaspoon cinnamon powder
¼ teaspoon turmeric powder
2 tablespoons olive oil

DIRECTIONS:

- Heat oil in the Instant Pot on sauté mode and fry garlic and onion for a minute.
- Add the tomato puree, salt, chili powder, and turmeric powder and fry again for 4-5 minutes.
- Add in the boiled meat and stir fry well on high heat for 10-15 minutes.
- Sprinkle cumin powder and cinnamon powder and mix well.

123.   Green Beans Tendered Beef
(Time: 120 minutes \ Servings: 4)

INGREDIENTS:

1 can green beans
½ lb. beef meat, pieces
2 tomatoes, slices
1 cup spring onion, chopped
1 teaspoon salt
1 teaspoon chili powder
1 teaspoon garlic powder
2 tablespoons olive oil
3 cups vegetables broth

DIRECTIONS:

- In the Instant Pot, add all ingredients and toss well.
- Cook on low heat for 2 hours on slow mode.

124.   Cauliflower Meat
(Time: 45 minutes \ Servings: 5)

INGREDIENTS:

½ lb. meat, beef, boiled
1 cup cauliflower florets
1 onion, chopped
2-3 garlic cloves, minced

2 tomatoes, chopped
¼ teaspoon turmeric powder
¼ teaspoon cumin powder
¼ teaspoon cinnamon powder
1 teaspoon salt
½ teaspoon chili powder
4 tablespoons olive oil
½ cup chicken broth
1 green chili

DIRECTIONS:

- Heat oil on sauté mode and fry the cauliflower for 3-4 minutes, set aside.
- In the same oil, fry onion for 1 minute. Add in tomatoes, chili powder, salt, and turmeric powder and fry.
- Now add the beef and the cauliflower and stir fry for 5-6 minutes. Add the chicken broth on and cook on manual mode for 10-15 minutes. Sprinkle cumin powder and cinnamon powder, toss well.

125. Beef with Pumpkin Bowl

(Time: 60 minutes \ Servings: 4)

INGREDIENTS:

½ lb. beef, boiled
1 cup pumpkin, peeled, chunks
½ teaspoons ginger paste
½ teaspoon garlic paste
1 teaspoon salt
1 onion, chopped
¼ teaspoon black pepper
2 cups chicken broth
3 tablespoons oil

DIRECTIONS:

- Heat oil in the Instant Pot on sauté mode and fry onion, ginger, and garlic for 5-10 minute.
- Add the beef, pumpkin, chicken broth, salt, and pepper and cook on slow mode for 50-60 minutes. Put in serving bowls and enjoy.

126.   Slow Cooked Beef Turnips

(Time: 70 minutes \ Servings: 5)

INGREDIENTS:

½ lb. beef, boiled
3 large turnips, peeled, diced
1 tomato, sliced
1 onion, sliced
1 teaspoon ginger paste
½ teaspoon garlic paste
1 teaspoon salt
¼ teaspoon chili powder
3 cups chicken broth
1 cup baby carrots
3 tablespoons oil

DIRECTIONS:

- In the Instant Pot, add all ingredients and mix well.
- Set on slow mode and cover with a lid.
- Cook for 60 minutes.
- Serve hot and enjoy.

127.   Fried Okra with Beef

(Time: 45 minutes \ Servings: 4)

INGREDIENTS:

¼ lb. beef, boiled, boneless
1 cup okra, sliced
1 tomato, chopped
1 onion, sliced
1 teaspoon garlic paste
¼ teaspoon ginger paste
¼ teaspoon turmeric powder
¼ teaspoon salt
¼ teaspoon chili powder
3 cups chicken broth
¼ cup olive oil

DIRECTIONS:

- Heat oil on sauté mode and fry okra until golden.
- Transfer to a platter and set aside.
- In the same pot, add onion and fry until transparent.
- Stir in garlic, ginger, tomatoes, salt, chili powder, and turmeric powder and fry for 6 minutes.
- Stir fry the beef for 5-6 minutes.
- Now add the fried okra and stir fry for 10-15 minutes.
- Sprinkle cumin powder and cinnamon powder.
- Transfer to a serving dish,.

128.   Beef Meat with Shallots
(Time: 20 minutes \ Servings: 3)

INGREDIENTS

¾ lb. of halved, peeled shallots
1 ½ teaspoon of olive oil
3 cups beef broth
¾ cup red wine
1 ½ tsp. tomato paste
2 lb. of trimmed beef tenderloin roast
1 tsp. of dried thyme
3 teaspoon of coconut oil
1 teaspoon of almond flour
salt and pepper, to taste

DIRECTIONS

- Heat the Instant Pot on medium heat and melt 1 teaspoon of olive oil. Sauté and season with salt and pepper.
- Roast the shallots and mix the wine and beef broth. Press Manual and cook the mixture on high pressure for 20 minutes.
- Close the lid, and when the timer beeps, quick release the pressure with a towel. Add the tomato paste. Pat the beef dry and sprinkle salt and pepper on it.
- Add the thyme, salt, pepper, and drizzle with coconut oil. Then pour ½ cup of water and sauté the beef on each side for 20 minutes. Once cooked, add the broth mixture, 1 ½ teaspoon of coconut oil, and the flour and cook on high pressure for 10 more minutes. Serve and enjoy!

129.   Cauliflower Rice with Ground Beef

(Time: 25 minutes \ Servings: 5)

INGREDIENTS

1 finely chopped onion
5 teaspoon of coconut oil
2 chopped cloves of garlic
2 diced tomatoes
1 pinch of salt
1 tsp. of sweet paprika
1 tsp. of saffron

2 cups cauliflower rice
3 cups beef broth
1 cup dry white wine
1 lb. of ground beef
1 tsp. of ground flax seeds
1 cup green beans

DIRECTIONS

-   Melt the coconut oil into the Instant Pot and sauté the onion until soft. Add the garlic, tomatoes, salt, paprika, saffron, and beans; then stir well and keep cooking until the tomatoes soften.
-   Add the ground beef and mix the ingredients. Add the cauliflower rice, broth, flax seed powder, and salt.
-   Close the lid and press the Manual to high pressure for 25 minutes. Once the timer beeps, quickly release the pressure.
-   Add the shallots and season with pepper and salt. Serve and enjoy!

130.   Sprouts with Pork Portions

(Time: 20 minutes \ Servings: 2)

INGREDIENTS

¼ lb. cubed pork
2 teaspoon coconut oil
1 lb. of halved brussels sprouts
½ chopped onion
1 pinch of salt or to taste
1 pinch of black pepper
1 tsp. flax seed powder
¼ cup toasted and chopped almonds
1 lemon zest
½ cup coconut milk

DIRECTIONS

-   Set the Instant Pot on medium heat and pour the coconut oil in it.

- Press Sauté and add the pork. Cook for 2-3 minutes.
- Add the onions, flax seed powder, and Brussels sprouts.
- Add ½ cup of coconut milk and set the Instant Pot to high pressure for 15 minutes.
- Season with pepper and salt. Serve the pork with the chopped mango and avocado with a handful of almonds and a squeeze of a lemon zest.

131.   Ground Beef with Flax Seeds

(Time: 30 minutes \ Servings: 2)

INGREDIENTS

2 lb. of ground beef	½ cup flax seed meal
1 package of sausage	½ tsp. of salt
2 tsp. of dried, chopped onion	1 tsp. of ground fennel
1 tsp. of garlic powder	1 cup dried slices of tomatoes
1 tsp. of dried basil	2 beaten eggs
1 tsp. of dried parsley	1 mango, cubed

DIRECTIONS

- In a deep bowl, mix the onion, garlic powder, dried basil, flax seed meal, salt, and ground fennel.
- Squeeze the sausage out of any casings and place in the bowl cut in very small pieces.
- Place the ground meat in the same bowl and mix the ingredients with hands.
- Shape the meat into the form of two loaves. Heat the Instant Pot on medium heat and melt a teaspoon of coconut oil. Transfer the meat loafs and press Meat/ Stew on high pressure.
- Close the lid and set the timer for 30 minutes.
- Serve the meat loaves with mango cubes.

132.   Veal Meat with Asparagus and Almonds

(Time: 20 minutes \ Servings: 3)

INGREDIENTS

1 lb. of veal meat
2 teaspoon of lemon juice
¼ tsp. of sea salt
1 pinch of ground black pepper

1 lb. of fresh and trimmed asparagus
2 teaspoon of coconut oil
6 cups mushrooms
½ cup green sliced onions
2 teaspoon of toasted and finely chopped almonds
3 cloves of minced garlic

DIRECTIONS

- Heat the Instant Pot and add ½ cup of water or coconut milk.
- Pour into the juice of 1 lemon, 1 teaspoon of oil, garlic, salt, and pepper.
- Add the mushrooms and veal meat.
- Close the lid of the Instant Pot and press the button stew mode for 15 minutes.
- Once the timer beeps, add a teaspoon of oil and asparagus and set on high pressure for 3 minutes.
- Release the pressure. Add the green onions and sauté for 2 more minutes.
- Remove the ingredients from the Instant Pot and pour over the lemon juice mixture.
- Serve the dish and enjoy with a sprinkle of almonds.

Seafood and Fish

133.   Lemon Fish Steaks

(Time: 25 minutes \ Servings: 3)

INGREDIENTS:

4 fish fillets
2 tablespoons extra virgin olive oil
1 teaspoon fine sea salt
1 teaspoon black pepper
Lemon wedges, for serving
2 tablespoons lemon juice

DIRECTIONS:

- Sprinkle salt and pepper on the fish. Drizzle lemon juice and oil, then rub all over.
- Place into a greased Instant Pot and cook for 15 minutes on pressure cooking mode.
- Serve with lemon wedges.

134.   Creamy Tilapia

(Time: 25 minutes \ Servings: 3)

INGREDIENTS:

½ lb. oz. tilapia fillets
2 tablespoons lemon juice
½ teaspoon of black pepper
2 tablespoons chopped fresh dill weed
½ teaspoon salt
Cooking spray

DIRECTIONS:

- Grease the Instant Pot with a cooking spray and place the fish filets, sprinkle salt and dill.
- Drizzle lemon juice and toss around. Roast for 20 minutes on pressure cook mode.
- After that, add cream cheese and black pepper and combine.
- Simmer for 2 minutes.

135. Roasted Fish with Vegetables

(Time: 25 minutes \ Servings: 4)

INGREDIENTS:

2 tomatoes, sliced
1 avocado, chopped
1 onion, sliced
1 bunch green coriander, chopped
½ cup tomato puree
1 teaspoon garlic paste
Salt and black pepper to taste
2 fish fillets, cut into pieces
1 teaspoon lemon juice

DIRECTIONS:

- Heat oil in the Instant Pot and fry garlic and onion for 1 minutes.
- Add the fish and fry until golden. Add tomatoes and keep frying.
- Season with salt and chili powder.
- Now add avocado, tomato puree, and lemon juice, simmer for 10 minutes.
- Sprinkle coriander.
- Transfer to a serving platter and serve.

136. Maple Zest Fish

(Time: 25 minutes \ Servings: 3)

INGREDIENTS:

2 fish fillets
4 tablespoons maple syrup
2 garlic cloves, minced
Salt and black pepper to taste
2 tablespoons soya sauce

DIRECTIONS:

- Heat oil in the Instant Pot and fry garlic for 30 seconds. Add the fish and sauté it for a minute or two.
- Season with salt and pepper. Drizzle maple syrup and soya sauce. Toss well. Simmer for 5 minutes.

137. Fried Fish Fingers

(Time: 25 minutes \ Servings: 3)

INGREDIENTS:

2 fish fillets, cut into 1-inch stripes
½ tablespoon salt
½ tablespoon black pepper
1 teaspoon garlic powder
3 tablespoons almond flour
1 teaspoon rosemary
Oil for frying

DIRECTIONS:

- In a bowl, add all the seasoning and mix well. Add in the fish fingers and toss well.
- Heat oil in the Instant Pot and fry the fish pieces until golden.

138. Fried Tuna with Tamarind Sauce

(Time: 25 minutes \ Servings: 3)

INGREDIENTS:

3 tuna fish fillets
2 tablespoons extra-virgin olive oil
1 teaspoon fine sea salt
1 teaspoon black pepper
Lemon wedges, for serving
2 tablespoons lemon juice

DIRECTIONS:

- Sprinkle salt and pepper on the fish. Then drizzle lemon juice and oil, rub all over the fish.
- Place it into a greased Instant Pot and cook for 15 minutes on pressure cooking mode. Serve with lemon wedges.

139. Fish Soul Satisfying Soup

(Time: 35 minutes \ Servings: 2)

INGREDIENTS:

1 teaspoon saffron
1 teaspoon garlic paste

Salt and black pepper to taste
2 fish fillets, cut into pieces
1 cup cream
1 pinch chili powder
1 cup full-fat milk

DIRECTIONS:

- Heat oil in the Instant Pot and fry garlic with onion for 1 minutes.
- Add the fish and fry well until golden brown.
- Season with salt and chili powder.
- Shred the fish with a fork and transfer back to the pot.
- Add in the cream and milk, mix well.
- Simmer for 10 minutes on low heat.
- Sprinkle chili powder and saffron on top while serving.

140.　　Fish with Tomatoes

(Time: 25 minutes \ Servings: 2)

INGREDIENTS:

2 fish fillets, cut into pieces
½ tablespoon salt
½ tablespoon black pepper
¼ teaspoon garlic powder
2-3 tomatoes, sliced
2 tablespoons oil

DIRECTIONS:

- Heat oil on sauté mode. Fry the fish until lightly golden.
- Season with salt, pepper, and garlic powder and add tomatoes.
- Cover with a lid and cook on stew mode for 15 minutes.

141.　　Salmon Bowl

(Time: 15 minutes \ Servings: 2)

INGREDIENTS:

2 salmon fillets, cut into pieces
½ tablespoon salt
½ tablespoon black pepper

¼ teaspoon garlic powder
1 cup lettuce leaves
1 tomato, chopped
2 tablespoons oil

DIRECTIONS:

- Heat oil on sauté mode. Stir fry the lettuce for 1 minute, then set aside.
- In the same pot, fry the fish until lightly golden. Season with salt, pepper and garlic powder.
- Transfer to a serving platter and s

142.   Fish Tamarind Gravy

(Time: 45 minutes \ Servings: 3)

INGREDIENTS:

3-4 fish fillets, pieces
½ tablespoon salt
½ tablespoon chili powder
¼ cup tamarind pulp
½ cup tomato curry
1 clove of garlic, minced
1 onion, chopped
Oil for frying

DIRECTIONS:

- Take a large bowl and put the fish fillets inside. Sprinkle salt and black pepper and place into a platter.
- Heat oil in the Instant Pot and fry the fish until golden. Cut into chunks and set aside.
- Then heat 2 tablespoons of oil on sauté mode. Add 1-2 tablespoons of oil, chopped onion, and garlic and stir for 1-2 minutes.
- Add the tomato puree, tamarind pulp, salt, and paprika, stir well and cook for 5-10 minutes on low heat.
- Now add the fish chunks and add ½ cup of water. Cover with a lid and cook for 5-10 minutes on manual mode. Transfer to a dish and serve.

143.   Teriyaki Salmon with Ginger

(Time: 10 minutes \ Servings: 3)

INGREDIENTS

¾ cup Kikkoman Teriyaki Marinade
¾ cup Teriyaki Marinade
2 teaspoon stevia
1 tsp. of grated fresh ginger root
4 salmon steaks
1 teaspoon of coconut oil

DIRECTIONS

- In a large bowl, combine the Kikkoman Teriyaki, marinade, stevia, coconut oil, and grated ginger root.

- Heat 1 teaspoon of olive oil in the Instant Pot and place the salmon. Pour the mixture over the salmon and press Sauté. Cook for 10 minutes. Serve and enjoy this healthy piece of fish.

144.   Salmon with Broccoli

(Time: 10 minutes \ Servings: 2)

INGREDIENTS

juice from 1 orange
1 teaspoon stevia
2 teaspoon soy sauce
1 teaspoon of coconut oil
2 Skinned and sliced salmon fillets
6 oz. of broccoli
4 oz. of topped and tailed green beans
2 peeled, stoned, and sliced avocados
6 halved cherry plum tomatoes
6 oz. baby spinach
2 oz. walnut halves
2 oz. almonds

DIRECTIONS

- Mix the orange juice, stevia, and soy sauce. Heat the coconut oil in the Instant Pot.
- Press Sauté and add the broccoli; stir for around 2 minutes.
- Add the salmon filets and the beans and sauté the mixture for 3 more minutes.

- Add the rest of the ingredients and keep cooking for 4 minutes with or without the lid. Serve immediately.

145.   Fish with Coconut and Cauliflower Rice

(Time: 25 minutes \ Servings: 3)

INGREDIENTS

2 teaspoon coconut oil
¼ cup chia seeds
3 thinly sliced onions
3 crushed garlic cloves
1 piece fresh peeled and finely grated ginger
2 teaspoon curry paste
1 can diced tomatoes
½ cup coconut milk
1 lb. white fish filets diced into2-inch pieces
½ cup frozen green beans
¼ cup fresh coriander leaves
Steamed cauliflower rice for serving
1 lemon cut into wedges

DIRECTIONS

- Heat the oil in the Instant Pot. Press Sauté and add the onion, then cook for 10 minutes on medium-high heat. Add the garlic and ginger and cook for several more minutes.
- Add the tomato and keep stirring until the ingredients are well combined.
- Add the coconut milk and a cup of cold water.
- Press Manual and close the lid. Then set on high pressure for 5 minutes.
- Once the timer beeps, add the fish and the green beans and keep stirring.
- Cook the ingredients for 10 minutes, loose lid.
- Once the fish is perfectly cooked, add coriander leaves.
- Serve and enjoy with the cooked cauliflower rice.

146.　　Tilapia with Chia Seeds

(Time: 15 minutes \ Servings: 4)

INGREDIENTS

½ lb. of tilapia filets
2 tsp. of coconut oil
3 teaspoon of chia seeds
¼ tsp. of Old Bay Seasoning
½ tsp. of garlic
½ tsp. of salt
1 sliced lemon
1 tsp. of grated ginger
1 package frozen cauliflower with red pepper and broccoli

DIRECTIONS

- Press Sauté and melt the coconut oil. Put the tilapia filets on the bottom.
- Season with the Old Bay and garlic, ginger, and salt and sprinkle chia seeds.
- Top each of the salmon pieces with lemon slices.
- Arrange the frozen vegetables around the portions of fish; season with salt and pepper.
- Cover the lid of the Instant Pot and set to high pressure for 10 to 15 minutes.
- Once the timer goes off, quickly release the pressure and enjoy this delicious dish!

147.　　Halibut with Blueberries and Sweet Potatoes

(Time: 15 minutes \ Servings: 3)

INGREDIENTS

4 Halibut steaks
4 Sweet potatoes
1 ½ cups frozen and fresh blueberries
2 teaspoon stevia
1 teaspoon coconut
zest of 1 lime
½ squeezed lime
1 pinch hot sauce
1 pinch black pepper
1 pinch flax seed powder
2 chopped mint sprigs

2 teaspoon fresh basil
1 pinch salt and pepper
3 teaspoon coconut oil
Arugula and Romaine with spinach for the salad

DIRECTIONS

- Cut the fish into small pieces and clean well.
- Melt coconut oil on a medium heat; then season the fish with salt, pepper, and ginger.
- Then, pu in the Instant Pot, and press Sauté for 5 minutes.
- Once cooked, remove the fish. In the Instant Pot, add the blueberries, lime zest, mint, pepper, ginger, mint, basil, flax seed powder, and potatoes.
- Pour 1 cup of water into the mixture and press Soup.
- Close the lid and set on high pressure for 5 minutes.
- Once the timer beeps, check if the mixture is thick; if not, cook for 5 more minutes.

148.   Scallops with Carrots and Ginger

(Time: 15 minutes \ Servings: 4)

INGREDIENTS

1 peeled and quartered carrot
1 quartered shallot
2 fresh peeled and thinly sliced
    ginger
2 halved garlic cloves
¼ cup white wine

1 cup chicken broth
1 teaspoon coconut oil
1 lb. sea scallops
a pinch of salt and fresh ground
    pepper
Snipped chives for garnish

DIRECTIONS

- Heat on medium heat and pour 1 teaspoon of coconut oil.
- Place the scallops in the Instant Pot and press Sauté.
- Cook for 4 minutes, flip once or twice and sprinkle salt and pepper.
- Once cooked, remove from the pot.
- Add in the carrot, shallot, ginger, e garlic, wine, and broth in the Instant Pot and cook for 10 minutes.
- Serve and enjoy the scallops with an avocado cream made of 1 peeled and sliced avocado, 1 teaspoon of coconut oil, ½ onion, and 1 pinch of salt.
- Sprinkle the scallops with chive.

Desserts

149.   Lemon Cake
(Time: 50 minutes \ Servings: 6)

INGREDIENTS:

2 cups coconut flour
2 tablespoons lemon zest
2 tablespoons lemon juice
1 teaspoon baking powder
¼ teaspoon baking soda
½ cup butter
1 pinch salt
4 eggs
1 cup coconut milk
1 cup stevia
½ cup stevia
½ cup apple jam

DIRECTIONS:

- In the Instant Pot, place a stand or a trivet and add 2 cups of water.
- Combine the flour, stevia, salt, baking powder, baking soda, eggs, lemon juice butter, milk, and 1 tablespoon lemon zest and beat with electric beater.
- Transfer to a greased baking pan and place on a trivet, cover and cook on pressure cook mode for 30-40 minutes. Combine the apple jam with stevia. Pour this mixture onto the cake and top with lemon zest.

150.   Chocolate Crackers
(Time: 40 minutes \ Servings: 6)

INGREDIENTS:

1 cup almond flour
1 cup cocoa powder
½ cup dark chocolate
½ teaspoon baking powder
½ cup butter
2 eggs

1 cup stevia

DIRECTIONS:

- Grease the Instant Pot with cooking spray. Combine all ingredients in a bowl and knead a soft dough.
- Roll out the dough on a clean surface. Cut with a cookie cutter.
- Place into the greased Instant Pot and cook for 30 minutes on manual mode.

151.   Pumpkin and Pineapple Cobbler
(Time: 50 minutes \ Servings: 4)

INGREDIENTS:

1 cup ripe pumpkin, peeled, chunks
1 cup pineapple, chunks
1 cup full-fat milk
½ cup stevia
1 teaspoon pumpkin pie spice
1 cup whipped cream for toping

DIRECTIONS:

- In the Instant Pot, add pumpkin, pineapples, milk, stevia, and pumpkin pie spice and cover.
- Cook on slow mode for 50 minutes. Put on a serving dish and top with whipped cream.

152.   Velvet Chocolate Pudding
(Time: 40 minutes \ Servings: 4)

INGREDIENTS:

1 cup dark chocolate, melted
1 teaspoon vanilla extract
1 cup cocoa powder
2 tablespoons butter
¼ cup stevia
½ cup dark chocolate sugar-free syrup
2 cups full-fat milk
2 eggs
½ cup dark chocolate chips

DIRECTIONS:

- Beat eggs until fluffy. In the Instant Pot, add butter and milk, then boil.
- Now add the cocoa powder and stir continuously.
- Add stevia and eggs by stirring gradually.
- Now transfer the melted chocolate inside and mix thoroughly.
- Transfer into a serving dish and place inside the freezer for 20 minutes.
- Drizzle chocolate syrup on top.

153.   Blackberry Smash

(Time: 40 minutes \ Servings: 4)

INGREDIENTS:

1 cup blackberries
2 tablespoons almond flour
1 cup full-fat milk
1 cup cream
½ cup stevia
2 tablespoons butter

DIRECTIONS:

- In the Instant Pot, melt butter on sauté mode. Add flour and stir well. Pour in the milk and stir continuously.
- Add in the cream, blackberries, and stevia, and cook on slow mode for 30 minutes.

154.   Pistachio Cake

(Time: 50 minutes \ Servings: 4)

INGREDIENTS:

2 teaspoon pistachio powder
4-5 tablespoons mint leaves, finely chopped
½ cup stevia
1 cup almond flour
1 teaspoon vanilla extract
1 tablespoon cocoa powder
2 eggs
½ cup butter

DIRECTIONS:

- In a large bowl, beat the eggs until fluffy.
- In another bowl, beat the butter with stevia, add vanilla extract and beat for 1-2 minutes.
- Now add it to the eggs mixture and almond flour, vanilla extract, mint leaves, and pistachio powder.
- Pour the butter into the greased Instant Pot and cover with a lid.
- Cook on pressure cook mode for 45 minutes.

155. Orange Flavored Cake
(Time: 23 minutes \ Servings: 3)

INGREDIENTS:

2 eggs
2 tsp. stevia
¼ teaspoon salt
2 teaspoon orange zest
2 cups heavy cream
1 teaspoon vanilla extract
2 cups almond flour

DIRECTIONS:

- Add eggs and stevia in a bowl. Mix in the salt, orange zest, heavy cream, vanilla extract and flour.
- Pour the batter into a round baking tray. Bake for 20 minutes into the instant pot.
- When ready, serve and enjoy!

156. Fruit Mix Dessert
(Time: 17 minutes \ Servings: 2)

INGREDIENTS:

2 cups almond flour
2 teaspoon baking powder
1 pinch salt
2 cups stevia
2 teaspoon butter
2 teaspoon vanilla extract
2 eggs

2 kiwi, sliced
2 cups strawberries, sliced
2 cups whipped cream

DIRECTIONS:

- Add flour and baking powder into a bowl. Mix in the salt, stevia, butter, vanilla extract and eggs.
- Pour the batter into a round baking tray. Cook for 15 minutes in the instant pot.
- When ready, spread whipped cream on the cake. Place kiwi and strawberries on top to serve!

157. Keto Carrot Pie

(Time: 40 minutes \ Servings: 4)

INGREDIENTS:

1 cup shredded carrot
1 cup full-fat milk
1 cup shredded mozzarella cheese
½ cup condense milk
1 teaspoon cardamom powder
4-5 almonds, chopped
4-5 pistachios, chopped
¼ cup stevia

DIRECTIONS:

- In the Instant Pot, place carrots, milk, condense milk, mozzarella cheese, cardamom powder, and stevia and cover. Cook for 40 minutes on slow mode.
- Transfer into a serving dish and top with chopped pistachios and almonds.

158. Coconut Milk Apple Crumble

(Time: 40 minutes \ Servings: 4)

INGREDIENTS:

1 cup apple, diced
1 cup coconut milk
½ cup stevia
1 tsp. cardamom powder
3-4 almonds, crushed

DIRECTIONS:

- In the Instant Pot add apples, coconut milk, cardamom powder, and stevia.
- Cook on slow mode for 40 minutes.
- When the apples are tender, smash with fork and transfer to a serving dish.
- Sprinkle almonds on top.

159.   Blueberry and Blackberry Cookies
(Time: 10 minutes \ Servings: 7)

INGREDIENTS

4 cups frozen blackberries
2 cups frozen blueberries
¼ cup stevia
2 teaspoon freshly squeezed lemon juice
2 teaspoon flaxseed meal
1 cup almond flour

DIRECTIONS

- Pour 2 cups of water and place the trivet/steaming basket inside. Grease the ramekins or the steel muffin cups with organic butter.
- Add the blackberries, blueberries, and stevia to a deep saucepan and cook the ingredients on low heat. Mix the lemon juice, flaxseed meal, and almond flour; then add to the berries and stir gently.
- Spoon the batter into the oiled ramekins and top with almonds.
- Press the setting button to high pressure for 10 minutes. When the timer beeps, naturally release the pressure and serve the cobblers.

160.   Chocolate Squares with Chia Seeds
(Time: 10 minutes \ Servings: 4)

INGREDIENTS

4 oz. dark chopped chocolate
1 ½ tsp. organic stevia
½ tsp. vanilla crème stevia
4 teaspoon of dried, diced mango
2 teaspoon of chopped almonds
¼ tsp. of chia seeds
¼ tsp. of coarse sea salt

DIRECTIONS

- Prepare the Instant Pot by pouring 2 cups of water and putting the trivet or the steaming basket inside.
- Grease the ramekins or the steel muffin cups with organic butter.
- Add the chocolate, stevia, and e vanilla crème stevia to heat proof ramekins; then stir to mix the ingredients.
- Immediately, pour the mixture to the ramekins and sprinkle the rest of the ingredients.
- Line the ramekins in the steaming basket.
- Set to high pressure for 5 to 10 minutes and close the lid.
- When the timer beeps, naturally release the pressure and serve!

161.   Pumpkin Cake

(Time: 10 minutes \ Servings: 10)

INGREDIENTS

3 cups almond flour
1 teaspoon baking powder
2 tsp. baking soda
2 tsp. ground cinnamon
1 tsp. ground nutmeg
½ tsp. ground cloves
1 tsp. ground ginger
1 tsp. salt
4 beaten eggs
2 cup stevia
1 can of pumpkin
1 cup coconut oil

DIRECTIONS

- Prepare the Instant Pot by pouring 2 cups of water and putting the trivet or the steaming basket inside.
- Grease a heat proof baking tray with organic butter.
- Then, sift the flour, baking powder, soda, salt, and spices all together in a bowl and set the ingredients aside.
- In a deep bowl, beat the eggs until you obtain a foamy mixture.
- Add the stevia and beat it until thick.

- Add the pumpkin and oil and beat again until the mixture becomes smooth. Blend the dry ingredients into the mixture of the pumpkin.
- Pour the batter into the already greased baking pan and press the setting high pressure for 10 minutes and close the lid.
- When the timer beeps, naturally release the pressure and serve the ramekins warm.

Made in the USA
Middletown, DE
25 October 2018